SWANSEA UNIVERSITY
PRIFYSGOL ABERTAWE
LIBRARY/LLYFRGELL

Classmark E176.1.P47 1984

Location

MINERS
LIBRARY

☆☆☆☆☆☆☆☆☆☆

George Washington (1789–97)
John Adams (1797–1801)
Thomas Jefferson (1801–09)
James Madison (1809–17)
James Monroe (1817–25)
John Quincy Adams (1825–29)
Andrew Jackson (1829–37)
Martin Van Buren (1837–41)
William Henry Harrison (1841)
John Tyler (1841–45)
James K. Polk (1845–49)
Zachary Taylor (1849–50)
Millard Fillmore (1850–53)
Franklin Pierce (1853–57)
James Buchanan (1857–61)
Abraham Lincoln (1861–65)
Andrew Johnson (1865–69)
Ulysses S. Grant (1869–77)
Rutherford B. Hayes (1877–81)
James A. Garfield (1881)
Chester A. Arthur (1881–85)
Grover Cleveland (1885–89)
Benjamin Harrison (1889–93)
Grover Cleveland (1893–97)
William McKinley (1897–1901)
Theodore Roosevelt (1901–09)
William H. Taft (1909–13)
Woodrow Wilson (1913–21)
Warren G. Harding (1921–23)
Calvin Coolidge (1923–29)
Herbert C. Hoover (1929–33)
Franklin D. Roosevelt (1933–45)
Harry S. Truman (1945–53)
Dwight D. Eisenhower (1953–61)
John F. Kennedy (1961–63)
Lyndon B. Johnson (1963–69)
Richard M. Nixon (1969–74)
Gerald R. Ford (1974–77)
Jimmy Carter (1977–81)
Ronald W. Reagan (1981–)

The Log Cabin Myth

☆☆☆

The Social Backgrounds of the Presidents

EDWARD PESSEN

Yale University Press
New Haven and London

Copyright © 1984 by Yale University.
All rights reserved.
This book may not be reproduced, in whole or in part, in any form (beyond that copying permitted by Sections 107 and 108 of the U.S. Copyright Law and except by reviewers for the public press), without written permission from the publishers.

Designed by James J. Johnson
and set in Aster Roman type by The Composing Room of Michigan, Inc.
Printed in the United States of America by
Vail-Ballou Press, Binghamton, New York.

Libary of Congress Cataloging in Publication Data

Pessen, Edward.
The log cabin myth.

Bibliography: p.
Includes index.
1. Presidents—United States—History. 2. Social classes—United States—History. I. Title.
E176.1.P475 1984 305′.93512 83–21887
ISBN 0–300–03166–1
0–300–03754–6 (pbk.)

The paper in this book meets the guidelines for permanence and durability of the Committee on Production Guidelines for Book Longevity of the Council on Library Resources.

12 11 10 9 8 7 6 5 4 3

UNIVERSITY OF WALES
LIBRARY
SWANSEA

To my dear grandchildren
Alex, Adam, and David—presidential timber, all

Contents

Preface

This book is about a surprisingly neglected theme. I decided to write it when I discovered that for all the many hundreds of books that had been published on different aspects of the American presidency, no study had yet been done on the presidents' social backgrounds and the implications of these backgrounds.

I became aware of this gap in the literature while doing research on the extent and significance of social mobility over the course of American history. I had meant to write a paragraph or two on the presidents as examples of upward mobility through politics, thinking I could pluck the appropriate generalizations from the writings on the subject. I discovered, to my amazement, that the bibliographical cupboard was bare. No serious study devoted to this not insignificant theme had yet appeared.

Sidney Hyman's valuable book on the presidency is one of the few scholarly treatises that touch on the theme, yet even it does so glancingly, in part of one chapter. Several reference books summarize the lives of the presidents from the cradle to the grave, but these compendiums are totally unanalytical, their evidence is thin, and they rely heavily on the unverified and often inaccurate essays by anonymous contributors to popular encyclopedias. (Thomas Reeves, author of a valuable biography of Chester A. Arthur, reports that one well-known encyclopedia has an entry on

Arthur that contains twenty-one factual errors.) When I say their evidence is thin, I mean, for example, that they settle for reporting that this or that president was a lawyer, without going into detail on whom he studied with or what law school he attended or precisely what kind of law he did and what kind of practice he had. In trying to place a lawyer in the American social structure, it makes all the difference in the world whether, in the era before law schools, he "read for the law" with a nonentity or a man of great eminence and whether his practice was characterized by servicing the claims of the poor or counseling the corporate mighty. The evidence on the careers of the presidents and their parents and grandparents is sufficiently detailed to enable us to probe beneath the general rubric "lawyer," but the popular reference books are indifferent to these crucially significant nuances.

The good biographies do, of course, contain much information on the social standing and material circumstances of the presidents and their families. But they are each concerned with their individual subjects—Dumas Malone with Jefferson, Douglas S. Freeman with Washington, Arthur Link with Wilson, to name three outstanding examples—not with the presidents as a whole. And I do not think it unfair to observe that even the most excellent presidential biographers have typically been indifferent to the possible significance of the rich social evidence they may have unearthed. Biographers of the presidents have not been students of the American social structure. Nor have they been interested in placing the presidents and their families on the appropriate level of that structure or in comparing the social standing of the presidents with the standing of the people or in mastering the theoretical literature on class and social structure the better to understand and treat the subject.

I have done a great deal of research in preparing this book but I have not tried to duplicate the work done by the thorough presidential biographers. While I have read the good biographies, I did not think it necessary to retrace the investigatory paths taken by Freeman, Malone, and Link, or Irving Brant on Madison, Charles Sellers, Jr. on Polk, the several excellent biographers of Jackson and Lincoln, Reeves on Arthur, Allan Nevins on Cleveland, Margaret Leech Pulitzer on McKinley, Henry F. Pringle and William H. Harbaugh on Theodore Roosevelt, Frank Freidel on Franklin D. Roosevelt, or Robert A. Caro on Lyndon Johnson. Since, for all their excellence, these and other reliable biographers are not as concerned as I with the precise social location of their subjects, I thought it necessary to examine many other sources in my attempt to compose accurate social portraits of the presidents. I discuss this literature and the sources on which this study is based in the short bibliographical essay at the end of the book.

I would add a few words on method. It has become increasingly modish for social and political scientists doing analytical studies to present their evidence and their argument in the form of tables, graphs, equations, statistical summaries. I prefer English prose to mathematical formulas. It is one thing to prepare a report on large segments of the population. It is quite another to report on only thirty-nine individuals. Who writes about so small a number of men has no excuse for falling back on the tables and graphs that are the stock-in-trade of those who have assembled fragmentary evidence on thousands. I have long thought and I continue to think it an imposition on readers to speak to them in jargon or an arcane tongue rather than in their own language. I think too that the most complex subject can be rendered in clear language. Certainly I have tried to do so.

I must mention the several people and institutions whose help and encouragement went far beyond the call of duty. Eric Spector and Jonathan D. Pessen were valuable research assistants during the early stages of the project. Adele Pessen did useful research on the social characteristics of the American people. "Inside information" was given me by John Niven and Donald B. Cole, each of whom has just completed a biography of Martin Van Buren, by Patricia P. Clark, associate editor of the Papers of Andrew Johnson project, and by the staff of Rosalynn Carter. Barbara Welter graciously shared with me the fruits of her research on the wives of the presidents. Edward Margolies offered an interesting thought about Ronald Reagan. Samuel Richmond brought a germane statistical theory to my attention. Bernard Barber and E. Digby Baltzell offered valuable evaluations and most encouraging appraisals of my theoretical discussion and analysis of the evolving American social structure. I learned a great deal from the responses to the lectures I gave on different aspects of the larger theme at the University of Toronto, the University of Notre Dame, the University of Kentucky, Fordham University, Baruch College, and the New York State Historical Association summer seminar at Cooperstown. Financial support from the Research Foundation of the City University of New York and the Guggenheim Foundation was indispensable. Altogether memorable were the five weeks I spent in 1978 as a resident scholar at the Rockefeller Foundation Center, the Villa Serbelloni, on Lake Como in Bellagio, Italy, where I first began to think seriously of writing this book. Fortunate is the author who is blessed with so wise an editor as Charles Grench and so gifted a copyeditor as Elizabeth Casey. If I have been able to work cheerfully and happily as well as steadily on this project, it is due largely to the friendly encouragement given me by my administrative colleagues at Baruch College—Joel Segall, president, Philip Austin, provost, and Martin Stevens, dean of liberal arts and sciences. Stan Buder encouraged me at an early stage to "drop everything and write this book." My greatest debt, as ever, is to my wife, Adele Pessen, whom I have doted and depended on since Franklin D. Roosevelt's time, for the good reason that, in the phrase of Johnny Mercer, she is too marvelous for words.

Brooklyn, New York
July 1983

EDWARD PESSEN

☆☆☆☆☆ CHAPTER ONE ☆☆☆☆☆

Introduction

In one respect, certainly, Phoebe Elizabeth Dickerson Harding of Blooming Grove, Ohio, seemed to be like mothers everywhere in the United States. Her great dream was that one day her son would grow up to become the president of the United States. In the enduring American legend, the rise to the presidency of so ordinary a boy as Warren Gamaliel Harding is yet one more proof that the greatest office in this nation is accessible to, and has in fact been occupied by, men born to modest circumstances. What greater tribute could there be to the socially democratic character of this country than that this lofty post—described by the eminent nineteenth-century English statesman John Bright as the "highest dignity, the finest spectacle, the greatest object of ambition in the whole world"—has regularly been attained by men of humble beginnings? At least, so goes the long-popular belief.

From George Washington's time to Ronald Reagan's, politicians, orators, editorial writers, ministers, and scholars have never ceased reminding us that the presidential race has typically been won by ambitious and hardworking men who reached the political heights primarily by their own heroic efforts. A typical newspaper editorial of one hundred and fifty years ago reminded readers that the lives of the presidents "serve as an example and incentive to the rising generation . . . as an evidence that honest labor is not degrading and that the highest civic honors are within the reach of the industrious and the persevering." A modern historian, writing a life of a president born to one of the wealthiest and most prestigious families in Virginia, claims to discern in that life "a familiar theme—the rise of a young man from relative obscurity to the highest position in the nation." The compiler of a recent government document on the lives of the chief executives reports that most of them were born in modest homes in "humble or middle-class surroundings." The author of a penetrating recent study of the powers of the presidency, glancing at the backgrounds of the men who have held the office, observes that "a self-made man" is one of the things that a candidate ought to be. And according to his most recent biographer, Theodore Roosevelt was only the exception in being born to comfort and wealth.

Who is of a mind to do so can extract dozens of similar testimonials from the record. While there can thus be no doubt of the pervasiveness and durability of this belief in the plebeian origins of almost all the presidents, there are reasons for grave doubt as to its accuracy. For it rests to a surprising extent on mere surmise or a hasty glance at the evidence. Perhaps because we have wished so hard to believe in the truthfulness of this political variation on the rags-to-riches theme, we have till now paid surprisingly little attention to the actual facts of the case.

As the most powerful and prestigious political office in the world, the American presidency has of course inspired a vast literature. Many hundreds of books and essays have been written about the nature and the powers of the office and its symbolic and other meanings, and almost as many publications have appeared on the thirty-nine individuals who have to date occupied the presidency. While these studies illuminate diverse facets of the office and answer many questions about it, they have almost entirely ignored one group of not insignificant questions. The aim of this book is to answer these questions.

Were the presidents typically born to parents and families of humble circumstances and modest station, as popular legend has it?

How do the material circumstances and social standing of the presidents' parents and grandparents compare with the standing and circumstances of the American people at different times in their history? Have the families of our top leaders been akin, socially and economically, to the families of the people they led?

Were the presidents upwardly mobile men before they attained the presidency? That is, how do their prepresidential careers compare with those of their parents and grandparents? (Or, in the cases of Jackson and Hayes, both of whom were born after their fathers died, how did their careers compare with those of the relatives who helped bring them up?)

What was the influence of their youthful circumstances and standing on their later achievements? To what extent did their beginnings account for whatever success they achieved as adults, in their careers and in the "good marriages" that so many of them made?

Finally, what is the significance, what are the implications of the evidence on the presidents' backgrounds? What light does it throw on their presidencies and on American politics? on American society and values?

These are the questions I consider in the pages that follow. One reason for previous neglect of these questions may be that we think we already have the answers to them. Among the most enduring and the most popular of American myths are those assuring us that our most exalted leaders, in politics as in business, have risen from the most modest beginnings, owing their success above all to their own ability and their own performance.

Sociologists and social historians have been disclosing for some time now that self-made businessmen are much more prevalent in American history textbooks than in American history. It remains to be seen whether most of the presidents were the self-made political men popular belief holds that they were.

Another possible reason for previous scholarly indifference to the theme of this book may be skepticism about its ultimate significance. In thinking about the presidency and the men who have held the office, most of us quite sensibly are concerned above all with what the presidents did during their administrations. It is their public deeds and the consequences of these deeds that affect our lives.

While we are curious too about the underlying causes of their behavior, we know that these causes are invariably many and complex. A crude economic determinism claims that men are motivated primarily if not entirely by their economic interests. A wiser view rejects so inflexible and mechanistic an interpretation. For we know of historic figures, some of them vastly influential, who, despite being born to wealth and privilege, nevertheless threw in their lot with the downtrodden of the earth. Man, as the Bible rightly says, lives not by bread alone. People are simply too complex, their thinking shaped by too many influences—tangible, intangible, rational, nonrational, selfish, unselfish—to be explained solely by their material interests.

Ah, but it is precisely because people are as complicated as they are that nothing about them or their experiences can be dismissed out of hand as possible explanation of their thinking and acting.

For surely it is possible that their material and social circumstances may throw some light on their behavior. If it is narrow economic determinism to interpret men's principles as a mere reflection of their material self-interest, it is equally narrow determinism to insist that their material and social circumstances have no effect whatever on their thinking and action.

No rigid formula equally applicable in all cases governs the relationship between circumstances and behavior. Some men may be totally indifferent to their interests in arriving at the policies they favor, others may be partially attuned to these interests, and others almost totally guided by them. A sensible rule is that there is no rule. The only way to find out the nature of the subtle reciprocity between condition and belief is to examine closely the evidence on each individual, in this case each president. That is what I have tried to do.

As is true of all questions that are not merely factual or tautological, the evidence can and will be interpreted differently by different observers. There can be no such thing, therefore, as a true or definitive interpretation. An intellectually stimulating interpretation would be achievement enough.

The evidence on the presidents' youth and later careers is important not only for whatever light it may shed on their social philosophies and presidential performance. It also speaks to the character of the American social and political systems or, more precisely, to the extent to which social democracy permeates the one and the other.

Students of human affairs since Aristotle's time have been curious about the material and social standing of political leaders. To judge by the many "quantitative studies" of the measurable characteristics of political leaders at all levels of government, in every state in the Union, and for all periods in our history, American scholars continue to be fascinated by the matter. True, as the political scientist Donald R. Matthews has observed, we have done very little with such evidence beyond gathering it. But we have indeed gathered much data and we have done so, I think, because we suspect that this evidence may turn out to be important. At the least, our data indicate, if *indirectly,* whether our politicians have been socially and economically representative of their constituencies. (They do so indirectly because the scholars unearthing them typically do no more than make inferences about the situation of "constituencies.") This book makes a direct comparison between our highest leaders and the led, for its portrait of the social and economic condition of the American people at different times in their history is based not on inference but on close examination of a variety of germane evidence.

If Americans lived in a truly classless society or one lacking important social and economic distinctions, the precise backgrounds of our political leaders would hardly matter. For, willy-nilly, they would be composed of the same social stuff as the people. But of course truly classless societies exist only in the minds of some men and women. Since American society, as I try to show in chapter three, has always been marked by important distinctions in the wealth, eminence, and influence of the families composing it, it becomes a matter of interest whether our highest leaders are a balanced cross section of our diverse and changing social order or atypical representatives of a small fragment of that order.

The discussion that follows engages these not inconsequential issues. And it attempts to respond to Professor Matthews's challenge by offering an interpretation of the significance of the social backgrounds of the presidents. It is more than time that we discover the extent to which one of our most influential myths is actually borne out by the facts of American history.

☆☆☆☆☆ CHAPTER TWO ☆☆☆☆☆

The Social and Economic Circumstances of the Presidents' Families

IN HIS CELEBRATED BOOK *The American Commonwealth,* James Bryce described the American presidency as "this greatest office, the greatest in the world, unless we except the Papacy, to which any man can rise by his own merits." As a wise man, the famed British visitor understood that a man's achievements were not necessarily dependent on his station in life. Rich men no less than poor or middle-class men could have the necessary "merits." But as a learned man and admired Catholic scholar, Bryce agreed with the conventional scholarly wisdom of his time that popes came almost invariably from the peasantry, in contrast to bishops and archbishops, who were with rare exceptions of aristocratic birth. In coupling the presidency with the papacy, Bryce was saying that America's chief executives had usually been men born to humble or modest status and condition. The point has been made so often, not only by Bryce and other foreign travelers but by articulate Americans as well, that it has come to be accepted by many as an article of the American faith. We have known that Washington, Jefferson, the two Roosevelts, and a few others were well born but we have liked to think that these presidents were atypical. But was this so? And has it been so in the century since Bryce visited the United States?

The belief in the humble origins of most of the presidents, for all its repetition and its popularity, has not been carefully examined, let alone proved, by the many orators, editorial writers, and political figures who have expressed it. In this chapter I shall try to answer questions about the presidents' origins by offering evidence on the social and material circumstances of the families into which they were born.

I have reserved for the third chapter my designation of the social class to which each presidential family belonged. Such designation is necessary if one means to compare the situations of the families of our top leaders with the situations of the families of the people they led. I trust it is not to give too much away at this point to observe that I divide the American social structure into six classes ranging from the upper upper class at the very top down through the lower upper, the upper middle, the lower middle, the upper lower, and the lower lower at the bottom. I shall of course offer my criteria for membership in these classes. Even before I do so, readers may find it instructive as they read the social vignettes presented in this chapter to place each presidential family within one or another of the six classes and then compare their rankings with mine. A cautionary note for those who intend to play this game may help them play it more effectively.

The social portraits that follow will allude regularly to presidential parents, grandparents, and ancestors who attended universities and were lawyers, doctors, and ministers, who owned thousands of acres and, if they were pre–Civil War Southerners, dozens of slaves, who freely spent thousands of dollars (many times more valuable than today's dollars) on other than necessities, who were influential in their churches and played active roles in local voluntary associations, and who held many public and government offices, whether as justices of the peace or as members of local and state legislative bodies. Many readers may conclude that these are commonplace attributes and achievements. Without venturing into the precise historical details, let it suffice for the moment to note that the next chapter offers chapter and verse revealing how highly atypical were and are even the most modest of the accomplishments cited in this brief catalogue.

In view of the wealth of social detail available for many presidential families, it would be possible to write a booklength manuscript on the theme of this chapter alone. I have necessarily been selective, focusing on those portions of a family's history that are suggestive of its social position. That the families do not receive equal space follows from the differing amounts of good evidence available for them. I have been inclined in some cases to include more rather than less, on the principle that symmetry be damned when the evidence on a particular family is illuminating and unusually interesting. In an attempt to place the circumstances of the presidents' families in clearer historical perspective, I have interspersed among the social portraits historical sketches that highlight important changes that occurred in American society.

In 1788 George Washington was elected the first president of the United States under the federal constitution that had gone into effect early that year. That constitution has come to be revered. Prior to its adoption, however, it split the nation into bitterly divided camps and was supported by a minority of the people. Few historians agree with Charles Beard's iconoclastic interpretation that the Founding Fathers who created the Constitution were motivated largely by the desire to enrich men like themselves by having the government under the new system honor at face value the much-depreciated notes in their possession. Equally few historians would deny that the new nation contained classes that differed drastically in wealth, status, and influence. White adult males were still denied the right to vote on grounds of property ownership and church membership. If possession of the suffrage was nevertheless far more widespread than "Progressive historians" two generations ago dreamed it was, politics as well as society were dominated by small numbers of men who vied among themselves to secure the greatest number of popular votes. The right to vote, as modern totalitarian states abundantly prove, was not the same thing as possession of political power.

As 1800 approached, blacks constituted almost twenty percent of the population. The overwhelming preponderance of the others were American-born persons of British descent. It was very much a man's world. The "female appendage," as many Americans regarded women, was supposed to live in order to marry and subsequently to preside over her small domestic world as men presided over the larger public world. Jefferson had written in 1776 that all men are created equal. In 1790 almost all blacks were slaves and most whites owned a tiny share of their communities' wealth. That commerce, finance, and manufacturing were important and gaining in importance, for all the era's preoccupation with agriculture, was shown by the policies supported by Alexander Hamilton, the first Secretary of the Treasury, who spoke for the Washington administration on these matters.

George Washington was the first and also the last president to be nominated without benefit of political party designation or support. All who followed as chief executive were nominated by one or the other of the two parties that have since the early 1790s dominated American politics: at first the Federalists and the Jeffersonian Republicans; then by the 1820s the National Republicans, soon followed by the Whig party, and the Jacksonian Democrats; and since the mid-1850s the Republicans and the Democrats. There is no suggestion that the presidential electors who chose Washington or the party caucuses and conventions that nominated all the other presidents were very much concerned about the social position of their candidates' families. As I shall try to show, they were interested rather in their candidates' attractiveness to voters and in their "soundness," whether in character or belief.

George Washington was born into a Virginia family of wealth and high distinction. A leading Washington biographer judges it an "honorable" family that performed the functions monopolized by "gentlemen" in that class-conscious society. Another notes that the family's repute was so high in what he calls that "semi-aristocratic society" that no social eminence was considered beyond Washington's rightful reach. The first of the family to come here was John Washington, son of an affluent minister, who emigrated from England shortly after the middle of the seventeenth century. (It should be kept in mind that if university attendance, professional status, wealth, and political influence were rare in the New World, they were even rarer in the Old.) The future hero's grandfather was a prestigious lawyer who left a substantial estate. Like other Washingtons after him, he abetted his career by marrying "above himself." His wife, George's grandmother, was the former Mildred Warner, the daughter of a gentleman who sat on the colony's exclusive royal council, a body accessible only to the crème de la crème of Virginia society.

Augustine Washington, George's father, was a planter and large landowner. Douglas Freeman has said of him that, at the time of his great son's birth, he was "not rich but he was prospering." The comment reflects Freeman's exaggerated notion of the kind of riches or property owned by most Virginians of the time. Augustine Washington owned forty-nine slaves and more than ten thousand acres during his son's early years. In the fashion of the era's leading men, he was active in his community as a church warden, sheriff, and executor of estates, duties that were reserved to men of high standing. The president's mother Mary Ball Washington was, in her infancy, willed an estate that later enabled her to live in comfort as the possessor of land, cattle, and slaves and to enjoy high social reputation. On her mother's death the young heiress was quickly accepted into a socially prestigious family that lived on a plantation near the Potomac.

The family of John Adams, the second president, was not nearly as wealthy as the Washingtons. And yet, at the time of John Adams's birth, it was hardly an undistinguished family. The problem was not in any lack of achievement on their part but rather in the modesty of the setting in which it took place. Bedeviling all attempts to place the Adams family—and several other presidential families—in their appropriate social niche is the fact that they were big fish but in a very small pond. In accord with the American penchant for downplaying the status of prominent men, his descendant Charles Francis Adams described the president's father, also named John Adams, as "a typical New England yeoman." The second president knew better. For, as he observed, "almost all of the business of the town was managed" by his father. The town in question, Braintree, may have been a veritable cradle of presidential families yet it was indubitably a small town.

The elder John Adams was a farmer but an unusual one, who continued the tradition of active public service begun by the first Adamses in the middle of the seventeenth century. The president's great-great-grandfather Joseph Adams had served the town as selectman and surveyor. Joseph Adams's great-grandson John Adams the elder was one of the pillars of the small community, perhaps the second among what a modern writer calls the "tribal elders" who monopolized its important offices. Lieutenant in the militia, deacon of the church, longtime selectman, the president's father was second in prestige only to Col. John Quincy, *the* great man of the town. (Adamses and Quincys were shortly to intermarry).

John Adams the elder married Susanna Boylston, whose grandfather was an eminent surgeon who had come to Massachusetts from London. It was this marriage into one of the leading families of the entire commonwealth that, according to the president, "lifted the Adams family of Braintree out of the obscurity of small town life," bringing what one biographer calls a "touch of sophistication into the family." Symbolizing the Adams family's lofty status in Braintree was its pew in the church, a structure that "measured the growth of social stratification in the community." At a time when the location of its pew reflected a family's social position in the community, the Adams pew, "located in a prized spot immediately to the left of the pulpit," proclaimed the family's towering status in the church and community.

With the election of Thomas Jefferson in 1800 a Virginian again occupied the nation's highest office. If Jefferson's great-grandparents were not at the very top of Virginia society, it has recently been established that they were much closer to it, much more prosperous and eminent, than had been believed. Accumulating land, slaves, and prestige, they moved the family forward "on the road to fortune and genteel station." The president's grandfather belonged to the gentry of Henrico County, where he was a captain of the militia and for almost twenty years a magistrate in the local court. By his time Jeffersons were members of the gentleman class, intermarrying with the colony's most distinguished families. Thomas Jefferson's grandmother Mary Field was the granddaughter of the speaker of the House of Burgesses.

The president's father Peter Jefferson became one of the leading landowners of Albemarle County, numbering among his thousands of acres the estate on which Thomas Jefferson would later build his great home at Monticello. A successful land speculator, Peter Jefferson acquired a fortune and enhanced his prestige by marrying Jane Randolph. After this marriage he became a lieutenant colonel, judge of the court of chancery of Albemarle, a member of the House of Burgesses, and was before his death regarded as the "chief officer and the first citizen of Albemarle County."

Jane Randolph Jefferson belonged to one of the leading families of that rarefied group known as the First Families of Virginia. Her father owned a vast plantation and estate, "Dungenes," in Tuckahoe. He served as adjutant general of the colony after winning acclaim for a "conspicuous military career." Her mother Jane Lilburne was a descendant of a famous English political leader of the early seventeenth century. The Randolphs were among a handful of Virginia families that combined baronial holdings with unsurpassed repute.

Jefferson's successor James Madison slightly undervalued what he called his own "paternal and maternal line of ancestry," saying of them that "they were planters and among the respectable though not the most opulent class." Like scholars of a later time, the fourth president exaggerated the numbers of contemporaries who were well-to-do. His most thorough biographer observes that the influential offices the Madisons held and their intermarriages with Virginia's leading families established the Madisons from "the earliest dates" as members of the colony's "ruling class."

The president's great-grandfather John Maddison [the original spelling] was a ship's carpenter who came to Virginia in 1653 and proceeded swiftly to buy up valuable landed property. His sons became large planters, held prestigious and influential positions, and married into the leading families in their communities. James Madison, Sr., the president's father, became one of the great land- and slaveowners of Virginia, owning more than five thousand acres of excellent land and over one hundred slaves. Upholding the tradition of service expected of men who had attained great material success, the elder James Madison became the commander of his county militia, justice of the peace, and a vestryman in his parish church. During the course of his life he came to be regarded as the "foremost 'squire' of the region." The president's mother Nelly Conway Madison was the daughter of one of Virginia's leading tobacco magnates. Her mother, after she was widowed, had married John Moore, a large planter.

The family of James Monroe, the last of the presidents of the "Virginia Dynasty," was prominent largely because of the status of the president's maternal line. Little is known about the Monroes other than what the fifth president himself recorded in a slim account he wrote after retiring from the presidency. Andrew Monroe came to Virginia from Scotland in 1650, according to a family tradition, after having fought two years earlier on the Royalist side in the famous battle of Preston. The several hundred acres he patented on both sides of "Monroe's Creek" were augmented manyfold over succeeding generations. The president's father Spence Monroe has been placed by a biographer in the class of the ruling gentry of Westmoreland County, where the Washingtons also lived, but at "the lower end of the scale." While Spence Monroe was not truly rich, he was prosperous enough to provide his son the finest kind of education and himself to ride, hunt, and pursue the other diversions characteristic of life among the gentry. Yet, while the president's father did have some slight public involvements, his record paled in comparison with James Monroe's great-uncle, Andrew, who, as a justice of the peace, colonel in the militia, and member of the House of Burgesses, performed the classic duties associated with a place in the Old Dominion's social elite.

The president described his mother Elizabeth Jones Monroe as "a very amiable and remarkable woman, possessing the best domestic qualities of a good wife and a good parent." She was also the daughter of the estimable James Jones, from whom she inherited much of "the considerable property" that he had amassed in

King George County, Virginia. When Spence Monroe died during the president's youth, his mother's brother Judge Joseph Jones assumed the responsibility for looking after him. James Monroe's uncle, whom he came to regard as his "second father," was a man of impeccable social credentials. Educated at the Inns of the Temple in England, Jones had a remarkably successful and varied career in Virginia. He served as the king's attorney for the colony, sat in the House of Burgesses, and during the Revolution was a member of the state's Committee of Public Safety and after the war a state supreme court judge.

John Quincy Adams succeeded Monroe in the White House. The great difference between the family status of John Adams and his son John Quincy Adams is that the latter was the son of a man who became president. Where John Adams's own father had been the second citizen of Braintree, Massachusetts, John Quincy Adams's father was the first citizen of the United States. Anyone who is familiar with his remarkable record of service, both before and after the presidency, cannot fail to be impressed with John Quincy Adams's superior abilities; anyone who is familiar with the lofty status, the comfortable conditions, and the great opportunities made available to the young Adams because of the political success achieved by his father cannot fail to be impressed with the significant role these advantages played in shaping John Quincy Adams's life.

Relative affluence, a cosmopolitan environment, and private schools in France and Amsterdam were the stuff of his youth. His mother Abigail Smith Adams was of a family that understandably felt that she could have done better at the time she married the future second president. Her father was the Rev. William Smith of Weymouth and her mother the former Elizabeth Norton Quincy of Mount Wollaston. In the phrase of one biographer, the Nortons and the Quincys "were powers in the Commonwealth." In the phrase of another, with John Adams's marriage to Abigail Smith, "a strain of aristocracy was now introduced into the Adams line." For both the Nortons and the Quincys could trace their ancestry back to families that had accompanied William the Conqueror when he left Normandy for England.

The election of Andrew Jackson in 1828 was then and later heralded as the rise of the common man. It used to be widely believed that the victory of this alleged commoner both symbolized and resulted from the extension of the suffrage to ordinary (white) men of little or no property. Historians have recently shown however that the expansion of the right to vote had occurred gradually and was well under way before Jackson's election. As a matter of fact, the implication that common men, once they won the right to vote, proceeded to reject "aristocrats" is a dubious one. It flies in the face of two kinds of evidence. The mass of plain citizens who esteemed the Virginians and the Adamses do not appear to have been particularly exercised about the social status of their favorites. And men every bit as "aristocratic" as the Virginia Dynasty continued to ascend to the nation's highest office during the "era of democracy." It is true that during the new age of *demagogy* that was ushered in with Jackson's election, rich and well-to-do candidates for the presidency (and lesser offices) began shamelessly to plead poverty and humble origins, under the evident conviction that voters would respond favorably to men of such background. The record indicates that in this, as in other ways, the politicians were doing American voters an injustice.

If the election of Jackson did not usher in democracy in America, a series of important technological and social changes did have a marked effect both on the nation's social structure and its politics over the course of the next generation. Revolutions in transport, communications, commerce, and production created vast new opportunities for the accumulation of wealth. The great increase in the nation's wealth masked what some scholars call appalling inequality. In towns and countryside in all sections of the United States, the new wealth was distributed more unequally than ever before. The mournful rule prevailed in pre–Civil War America that the rich became richer, owning an increasing proportion as well as amount of the total, while the poor became more numerous. Cotton production spurted, spurred at the source by the development of the cotton gin and at the manufacturing end by the spread of power-driven textile machinery located in factories. Motivated in part by their fear that the spread of the factory system would devalue their skill and in part by their worsening standard of living, skilled artisans and mechanics in most of the nation's towns and cities formed trade unions combining skilled members of different crafts in single citywide organizations. Although many of their hundreds of strikes for a shorter working day than the traditional "sunup to sundown" were successful, the labor movement collapsed during the depressions that followed the financial panics of 1837 and 1857. Labor's political weakness was manifested in the quick snuffing out of the Working Men's party and by the hostility shown by state courts to the very idea of the closed shop. An "urban revolution" helped lure armies of German and Irish Catholic immigrants to this country, accentuating inequality and heightening social tensions between the newcomers and white-skinned natives.

The years 1830–1860 have been called an age of reform, since voluntary associations dedicated to amelioration of the lot of slaves, prisoners, the poor, women, orphans, the culturally deprived, the congenitally enfeebled, and other of society's victims flourished during the era. One reason for the proliferation of these high-minded but not impressively effectual organizations was precisely the major parties' indifference to social problems. For a variety of reasons, not excluding their support by the most influential and powerful elements in American society and their access to ample funds, the major parties thrived, monopolizing high political office and easily brushing aside the challenges of a number of short-lived "third parties," organizations that were short-lived because they were dedicated to principle in a country that had come to prefer the politics of pragmatism.

☆☆☆

Andrew Jackson or "Old Hickory" as he was affectionately known has long been regarded as the first true commoner to rise to the highest office. He was ostensibly the pioneer in an almost unbroken line of subsequent presidents of plebeian or humble origins. That line, as we shall see, was far from unbroken. And there is some question as to the accuracy of the myth that assigns Jackson's family to the lower orders.

In describing Andrew Jackson as "the absolute personification of the self-made man," a modern biographer points out that he had "no father [and] no family to speak of." His father died before the seventh president was born. But as for family, an earlier biographer noted that few families who came to this country in the 1760s could look "forward to the prospect of starting life in the New World under the sponsorship of so large a colony of kinfolk and connections as received the Andrew Jackson's" in South Carolina. (The reference is to Old Hickory's father who, as was true for numerous other presidents' fathers, bore the same first name as his son.) The elder Andrew Jackson was the son of a relatively successful Irish weaver and merchant. Rejecting his father's offer of an apprenticeship, the elder Andrew and his wife Elizabeth Hutchinson Jackson decided to join four of her married sisters in Mecklenburg province where the Jacksons settled on two hundred acres. The infant Andrew was taken by his mother to live in the home of one of these sisters, Jennet Crawford. Her husband, James Crawford, the head of the household in which Andrew Jackson was brought up, was described by a reliable contemporary as a man of "considerable substance." Crawford was a well-to-do land- and slaveholder who owned a fine home, a gristmill, and a still for making whiskey, among other valuable properties. According to his most thorough modern biographer, it was among the aristocracy of backcountry North and South Carolina, "the owners, the breeders of horses, the holders of local offices and titles [that] Andrew Jackson was born and spent his life." When he was fifteen his merchant grandfather left Jackson a legacy of between £300 and £400. This youth attended a private academy, while enjoying "many advantages" unknown to the great mass of young Americans of his age.

Martin Van Buren, Jackson's handpicked successor in the White House, came of a family whose status appears to have been as close to the Jacksons and the Crawfords as the politics of "little Van" were to those of Old Hickory. Having read the available biographies of Van Buren and consulted with the surprisingly large number of authors—five—who have been preparing new biographies or collections of the papers of the eighth president, I think it safe to say that we know little about his family beyond what Van Buren himself has told us. In the autobiography that he wrote in his retirement, Van Buren said that his great-great-grandfather left Holland in 1633 to settle in Rensselaer County in what was later New York State. The president's great-grandfather, also named Martin Van Buren, moved to Kinderhook and "settled on lands conveyed to him in 1669." Although Van Buren claimed that his father Abraham Van Buren was "utterly devoid of the spirit of accumulation," he noted that his father nevertheless kept adding to his "originally moderate" property. A farmer and an owner of a tavern in Kinderhook, at a time when tavern ownership was a privilege conferred only on respected community leaders, Abraham Van Buren was a captain in the militia during the Revolution, became a prosperous property owner, and, according to Donald Cole, the modern student who seems most conversant with the president's early life, was "a prominent figure" in the community. He belonged to that small group who in 1790 owned more than five slaves. He indeed held that "respected position" in society attributed to him by his famous son.

Mary Hoes Van Buren, the president's mother, was of a family long prominent in Holland, where their name originally was Goes (the name too of the great Renaissance painter). The Hoeses were among the first patentees of Kinderhook. The president's maternal grandfather Johannes Dirkse Hoes was one of the largest taxpayers in Kinderhook. Mary Hoes's first husband Johannes Van Alen was a man of high standing and her son of this marriage, James I. Van Alen, the president's half brother, became a distinguished lawyer, a judge in Columbia County, and a United States congressman.

When William Henry Harrison—or "Tippecanoe," as he was popularly known, after the scene of his well-known military exploit—ran for president in 1840, his party managers exploited a boner by the opposition to tell the country that their candidate was used to living in a simple log cabin and was a man of humble origins. Actually, the president spent his childhood on a truly lavish plantation, attended by corps of slaves and servants. The disparity between reputation and reality in this case is so glaring that I cannot forbear paying particularly close attention to Harrison's lineage. No presidential family surpassed and few could match the status of the Harrisons.

Nothing is known of them in England. A great deal indeed is known of them, however, after they arrived in Virginia early in the seventeenth century. A brief recapitulation of the achievements of and the eminence earned by the president's ancestors over five generations suggests their unexcelled standing. The first Benjamin Harrison amassed large properties on both sides of the James River and was active in the colony's public affairs. In succeeding generations the oldest son was given the name Benjamin as well as the lion's share of his family's continually expanding estate. The president's great-great-grandfather, the second Benjamin Harrison, sat for many years in the House of Burgesses, was a member of the original board of governors of William and Mary College, and for twelve years sat on the royal council of Virginia. His eldest son became the attorney general of Virginia, after having served in the Burgesses and as speaker and treasurer of the colony. The president's grandfather, the fourth Benjamin Harrison, served only in the Burgesses, for he presided over an estate so huge that administering it appears to have occupied most of his time. He married Anne Carter, the daughter of the wealthiest native-born American. Harrisons had by then entered into marriages with such Virginia families as the Randolphs, Lees, Wythes, Blands, Carys, and Pendletons, as well as Carters, so that there was "scarcely a prominent man in the colony" to whom the president's father, the fifth Benjamin Harrison, "could not claim some degree of kinship."

A wealthy slave- and landowner who at age 19 inherited six plantations from Benjamin Harrison IV, the president's father managed to win reelection to the House of Burgesses for almost twenty-five years prior to the outbreak of the Revolution. During the fighting he played a leading part in the committees that ran Virginia and he was three times governor after the fighting stopped. As for the president's mother, the former Elizabeth Bassett, her family's standing rivaled that of the Harrisons. The family of her mother, Elizabeth Church Bassett, was bound by ties of marriage and social intimacy to "half the most prominent Virginia families."

The other half of the Whig party slate of "Tippecanoe and Tyler too" was John Tyler who, barely one month after Harrison's inauguration, found himself the nation's tenth president. Like the Harrisons, the Tylers belonged to that roster of patricians known formally as the First Families of Virginia (FFV). A family tradition claimed that a Tyler had accompanied William the Conqueror from France to England in the eleventh century. What is more certain is that from the time of Henry Tyler, who emigrated from England in the middle of the seventeenth century, the family accumulated substantial landed and slave property in addition to "prominence in the community." The community in this case was the prestigious "Peninsula," the cluster of counties between the James and York rivers. The president's father Judge John Tyler was a wealthy man who owned several large plantations. When he was a boy the president lived in "Greenway," the manor house of one of these plantations, on a 1200-acre property attended by forty slaves. Educated at William and Mary, Judge Tyler had studied law under the eminent Robert Carter Nicholas. After serving eight years in the Virginia legislature, four of them as speaker, he became a judge of the state court of admiralty, was for twenty years a judge in the highest criminal court, and was elected and reelected governor of Virginia for three successive terms. At the time of his death he was a judge of the United States District Court for Virginia. His wife was Mary Amistead Tyler, the daughter of a prominent planter.

Tyler was succeeded by James Knox Polk. Polk's father Sam Polk had lived in a log cabin, but it was a cabin of the "saddlebag" type that, according to a modern historian, denoted "well-being" in early Mecklenburg County, South Carolina, where young James was brought up. Sam Polk's father Col. Ezekiel Polk was the founder of Mecklenburg. No less an authority than George Washington had noted "the very rich look" of the bottomlands owned by Sam Polk. Brother to the fabled land speculator William Polk, who was the richest man in the county, Sam Polk was himself an unusually well educated commercial farmer, a large land- and slaveowner, and a banker who speculated successfully, if not on as grand a scale as did his brother. A man with "a passion for the world's goods," Sam Polk acquired a fine house on the most fashionable street in Columbia, South Carolina. The dimensions of his fortune are suggested by the $40,000 that at one point in his career he and a partner invested in building a steamboat. Sam Polk's high standing resulted not only from the size of his holdings and the scope of his enterprises but from his service as a major in the militia, justice of the peace, and city magistrate. His wife Jane Knox Polk was a descendant of the great Scottish religious reformer. Her father owned considerable real estate and many slaves, was admired for his piety, and was regarded as one of the leading citizens in the community.

The twelfth president, Zachary Taylor, was the ninth who was a Southerner. The "log cabin tradition" of Taylor's birth, according to his leading biographer, "paints a perverted picture of his parents' financial and social status, for his birthright was the manor house and not the low log hut." A Taylor came over on the *Mayflower* and from early in the seventeenth century the Taylors had earned a place "high on the colonial scale" among the First Families of Virginia. Zachary Taylor was a second cousin to James Madison by virtue of the marriage of his grandfather's sister to Ambrose Madison. Living in splendid homes, the Taylors owned thousands of acres of real estate and slaves on many plantations. The president's father Richard Taylor owned two dozen slaves on his Virginia property and more than ten thousand acres in Kentucky. Like other members of the Virginia social elite, Taylors complemented their wealth with respected if modest social service. Richard Taylor was a lieutenant colonel, justice of the peace, and county magistrate. The president's mother Sarah Dabney Strother Taylor grew up amidst elegant surroundings and was educated by tutors who had been imported from Europe. When she was left motherless during childhood, she went to live with her cousins in Culpepper County, Virginia, in the home of her uncle, a prominent man who had signed one of the first protests against the Stamp Act.

In Millard Fillmore, who became president on the sudden death of Zachary Taylor in 1850, the nation for the first time had a president who had been born in a crude log cabin. In his reminiscences, Fillmore wrote that at the time of his birth his parents and his uncle and aunt "occupied the same log house, in the midst of the forest, having no neighbor nearer than four miles." The surrounding farm occupied four hundred acres, a modest holding compared to those of earlier presidents' families. Nathaniel Fillmore, the president's father, was a Vermont farmer who, with his brother, had been lured to Cayuga County, New York, by glowing accounts of prospects there. The president's mother, the former Phoebe Millard, had been brought up in comfortable surroundings in Pittsfield, Massachusetts, where her father was a doctor. When she was about sixteen she fell in love with Nathaniel Fillmore and shortly thereafter wed this "adventurous farmer," who is described by one biographer as a man "whose boldness outstripped his ability or at least his luck."

Gen. Benjamin Pierce, the father of Franklin Pierce, was one of the pioneer settlers of Hillsborough, New Hampshire, earning local fame as a Revolutionary War hero. Like the elder Van Buren, a farmer and a tavern keeper, the general was not a rich man but he was a prosperous one. He lived in a large and impressive house, was known as a generous "squire," famed for his hospitality, and he was capable of sending his son to private tutors and to Bowdoin College. His reputation as *the* personage of rural Hillsborough was earned by his diverse services to the community, ranging from county sheriff, delegate to the state council, and representative to the state legislature. After Franklin's birth his father was elected governor of the state. Little is known of the president's mother, apart from his own not very gracious comment that he attributed his tendency to drink excessively to "maternal example."

James Buchanan succeeded Pierce in the presidency. Buchanan's father, also named James, was one of three presidential fathers born abroad (all in Ireland), the son of John and Jane Russell Buchanan. Orphaned at an early age, the elder Buchanan was brought up by his mother's family, who provided him "a good home and a good education." In 1783 when he was twenty-two he emigrated to Pennsylvania, where he stayed for a while with his mother's uncle, Joshua Russell, a wealthy "man of consequence." The president's father did well in business, his success with a warehouse and a trading post enabling him to build a fine two-story brick house on a "splendid 300-acre tract," and to send his son to a private academy. His business success combined with his community service as a justice of the peace won Buchanan the esteem of his contemporaries as "one of the most prominent citizens" in Mercersburg, Pennsylvania. Elizabeth Speer Buchanan, the president's mother, was the daughter of James and Mary Paterson Speer, Scottish Presbyterians who had emigrated to Pennsylvania in 1756. Little is known of her apart from her son's remark that she was an unusually well-read and remarkable woman, particularly in view of her "limited opportunities in early life," when she evidently worked hard on her parents' farm.

In popular legend, the sixteenth president is the quintessential example of the rise from rags to renown. Despite the fact that few men have been the subject of as many books as Abraham Lincoln, surprisingly little is known about his ancestors. Lincoln himself was able to trace them only to his paternal grandfather, also named Abraham. Later investigators traced the family to Samuel Lincoln, an apprentice weaver, who emigrated from England to Hingham, Massachusetts, in 1637. A modern historian reports that Lincoln's forebears earned a good living and the respect of their neighbors. The sixteenth president's grandfather is described by Carl Sandburg as a militia captain who owned a 200-acre farm in Rockingham County that had been deeded him by his father John Lincoln. Described elsewhere as a "prosperous pioneer farmer," it was this grandfather who in 1782 brought the family to Jefferson County, Kentucky, twenty miles east of Louisville.

His son Thomas Lincoln, Abraham's father, has often been described as a lazy and shiftless failure, a man who supposedly represented a distinct falling off in the quality of the Lincoln line. When he achieved national prominence Abraham Lincoln said,

"It is a great piece of folly to attempt to make anything out of my early life. It can all be condensed into a single sentence and that sentence you will find in Gray's *Elegy*—'the short and simple annals of the poor.'" Actually, as the most recent Lincoln biographer points out, Thomas Lincoln "enjoyed considerable status" among his neighbors in Indiana, where he moved the family when Abe was a boy. He served on county patrols, sat on juries, guarded prisoners, and appraised estates. Coming from a family of small slaveowners, Thomas Lincoln was a skilled carpenter as well as a farmer. At the time of his great son's birth, he owned two farms of six hundred acres, several town lots, livestock, and horses, property that was quite close to the total owned by the wealthiest man in the area. Five years later he belonged to the richest fifteen percent of taxpaying property owners in his community.

Of his mother, Nancy Hanks, Abraham Lincoln said little other than that she was born in Virginia. If his law partner Billy Herndon can be believed, Lincoln told him he thought Nancy Hanks had been born out of wedlock. The Hanks genealogy has been described as a "confusing wilderness that most scholars despair of ever penetrating." Since she died when she was only thirty-one, her son's description of her as a "wrinkled woman" with "withered features" and "a want of teeth" suggests something of her toilsome life. When Abe was ten his father married Sarah Bush Johnson, the widow of the county jailer. This kind and cheerful—and illiterate—woman was to be remembered by Lincoln as his "good and kind mother." Whatever their personal qualities may have been, neither Nancy Hanks nor Sarah Johnson appears to have contributed very much to the social status of the president's family.

Andrew Johnson succeeded to the highest office after the assassination of Lincoln. Very little is known about Jacob Johnson, the seventeenth president's father, and even less about his paternal ancestors. Jacob Johnson is described by the modern editors of Andrew Johnson's papers as an obscure and "unskilled man-of-all-work," whose jobs ranged from janitor through bank messenger and porter. An early biographer described Jacob Johnson as a poor man, but he did so on the dubious premise that the pre–Civil War South had no middle class to speak of: men were either well-to-do slaveowners or poor whites. While the elder Johnson owned a simple two-story house in Raleigh, North Carolina, he was hardly a rich man. If his jobs were only slightly higher than menial, he appears nonetheless to have been on strangely familiar terms with the city's most influential and prestigious men, Dr. William G. Hill, Col. Thomas Henderson, editor of the *North Carolina Star,* and Col. William Polk, uncle of President James K. Polk, who was said to have arranged Johnson's bank job for him. It is possible that Johnson's "eminence" owed much to the fact that he had heroically saved Henderson from drowning, and something to the fact that later eulogists may have sought to romanticize, if not glorify, a president's father. The fact remains that Jacob Johnson had managed to become a captain of the city watch or local constabulary—if not, as one biographer erroneously identified him, a captain of a militia division—as well as a sexton in the local Presbyterian church and the town crier; moreover, he won a reputation among his contemporaries as "the best-loved person in town."

His wife Mary McDonough Johnson was the daughter of Andrew McDonough, a veteran of the Revolutionary War and cousin of Commodore Thomas McDonough, who achieved fame in the War of 1812. Other claims to eminence for Andrew Johnson's maternal line are undocumented and unproven.

The first president elected after the Civil War, Ulysses S. Grant owed his rise to his victories as a Union general. For that matter, most of the men who followed him into the high office during the remainder of the nineteenth century capitalized politically on their exploits during the war. The nation changed drastically in the half century after the Civil War. The factory system and power-driven machinery triumphed decisively over all other forms of industrial production. Farmers too relied increasingly on an expensive technology that among other things put them in debt to anonymous outsiders. The new forms of corporate enterprise that administered the factories and the nation's almost completed railroad network were dominated by businessmen and investment bankers who commanded the necessary resources of capital. These giants of finance seemed in some instances to control politics with as much ease as they ruled the nation's economic life, casually flicking aside the slight restraints and penalties called for in the era's feeble antitrust laws and its attempts at business regulation. Armies of cheap and for the most part docile immigrant laborers poured into this country from southern and eastern Europe, flooding the cities that by the era's end for the first time came close to matching the population of the countryside. The weakness of the era's trade unions (for all their dramatic strikes and occasional violence), like the poignant but ineffectual attempts by farmers to restore the conditions of a more roseate past, pointed both to the weakness of the nation's laboring classes and to a growing imbalance of power in American society.

Blacks had early in the postwar period won the right to vote and to hold office, as well as to equal protection of the laws. But these theoretical rights were brushed aside by white society, particularly in the South. The social and economic as well as the political status of blacks in the late nineteenth century deteriorated to what some black historians refer to as the "nadir" in black history in the United States.

Despite all the changes induced by the sweeping technological developments of the era, the social structure remained sharply differentiated. If anything, the gulf between the classes widened and the proportions of the population enrolled in the lower classes increased. In many communities, great numbers of individuals did improve their lot, occupationally, throughout the later nineteenth century and for much of the twentieth. This mobility across the occupational structure was the sort sociologists call "short-distanced," representing modest gains for those experiencing it. It neither dissolved class differences nor lessened the barriers between the classes. In Theodore Roosevelt's time as in Ulysses S. Grant's, the families of presidents, like the families of other Americans, continued to belong to one or another class within what continued to be a stratified society.

Ulysses S. Grant was born into a family that, in its male line, had been in this country since 1630, when Matthew and Priscilla Grant left England for Dorchester, Massachusetts. Six generations of Grants lived and held a respected place in their New England, mainly Connecticut, communities. The second Noah Grant was killed in battle during the 1750s and his son, the future president's grandfather, is said by some Grant biographers to have fought for six years on the patriot side during the American Revolution. This Grant, the third Noah, although imprisoned for a short time because of his failure to pay a debt of slightly more than £50, evidently had enough property from his land speculations to raise almost £100 from the sale of some of his lands before he moved west with his wife, Rachel Kelly Grant. The president's father Jesse Root Grant was apprenticed at age 11, shortly after his mother's death, to a man who was fairly prominent in his Ohio community. Although he received only a slight education, Jesse Grant prospered after joining his half brother Peter Grant in the tanning business. By the time the future president was born, his father had become the richest man in Ravenna, a community that contained substantial merchants, professionals, and artisan-entrepreneurs, as well as laborers. A recent biographer writes that Jesse Root Grant "married up," when he won the hand of Hannah Simpson, daughter of a prosperous farmer, John Simpson, who had recently paid \$3600, an unusually high sum for that time, for his 600-acre farm in the Ohio Valley. John and Rebecca Simpson, unlike the Grants, were "lettered people" with a claim to "gentility." Described by the most recent Grant biographer as a member of the "small town bourgeoisie," Jesse Root Grant was active in politics, first as a Jacksonian, later as a Whig; he served one two-year term as mayor of the town of Georgetown, and was also a master of a Masonic lodge.

Grant's successor was Rutherford B. Hayes. Like Andrew Jackson before him, Hayes was born shortly after his father died. Hayes descended from a family that emigrated from Scotland to Connecticut in 1680 and shortly afterward moved to Vermont. An early biographer describes them as "strong, solid men of the best New England sort" (whatever that may mean). The future president's grandfather married into an upper-class family. His son, the president's father, achieved success in Vermont, where he was known as Rutherford Hayes, Esquire, before moving to Ohio in 1817. There he thrived as a distiller, real estate investor, and importer. He built the first brick house in Delaware, Ohio, a home that was better and "more genteelly furnished" than those of his neighbors. He was a leading church member and a prominent citizen, admired for his business success and his lifestyle. His wife Sophia Birchard came of a family that had settled in Norwich, Connecticut, in 1635. She was the granddaughter of a Revolutionary War veteran—even if he was not the "officer under General Washington" that he claimed to have been. Her father owned a number of farms and doubled as a retail and importing merchant.

Rutherford B. Hayes was looked after financially by his mother's brother, Sardis Birchard, whom Hayes came to regard as his "true father." Birchard was a partner in what in the 1830s was the largest merchandising house in Cleveland and he was so successful a land speculator that after 1839 he was "independently wealthy for life." What was until then the nation's worst depression, in the years following 1839, held no terrors to the man known to the Seneca Indians as "An-Se-Quag, the man who owned most of the land." Hayes grew up under the tutelage of this wealthy man who was reputed to enjoy "one of the widest circles of influential acquaintances in Ohio."

James A. Garfield, the twentieth president, was to comment late in his life: "I lament sorely that I was born to poverty." A leading biographer's observation that Garfield's complaint was "not quite fair" seems to be borne out by the evidence. While the historical record is silent about the kind of social prestige enjoyed by Garfield's paternal line after Edward Garfield left England for Watertown, Massachusetts, in 1635, the data for his maternal line, the Ballous, are more abundant. Arriving here exactly fifty years after the Garfields, the Ballous became "noted clergymen and educators."

The president's father Abram Garfield was born at the end of the eighteenth century in Worchester, New York. In a pattern that was characteristic for rural families of the time, he was apprenticed as a boy to a farmer in northern Ohio. After being orphaned, he spent his early manhood working extremely hard before marrying Eliza Ballou at age twenty and moving west with her to a log cabin on the Cuyahoga River. Living as the new family did in an economically stagnant and disease-ridden area, life was hard and punctuated annually by sickness. By the time James Garfield was born, however, his family was thriving, if modestly, as a result of his father's distinctive assets—his great strength, his flair for hard work, his personableness. He managed to save enough money, in part from a profitable canal-building venture, to buy a parcel of land and move the family into what the future president later recalled as "the first land and house we ever owned." Abram Garfield was in fact doing comparatively well in his community before he died. Indignantly denying that the Garfields were poor, the president's mother Eliza Ballou Garfield said, "We lived as well as our neighbors." Her definition of a poor family was one that did not pay its debts, lived on charity, was shiftless, and not respected by its neighbors. The Garfields were none of these and could therefore "look any man in the face." By his own account, the president, when he was a boy, ate remarkably well, did not have to do the chores normally required of a youngster on a farm, and had an unusually good education.

The assassination of Garfield thrust Chester A. Arthur into the presidency. His father William Allen Arthur was of Scots-Irish descent and, like the fathers of Jackson and Buchanan, was born in Ireland. William Arthur was never a rich man but he had, by the time of his son's birth, become a fairly eminent and a most respected man. Although of a rural Ulster family, the elder Arthur attended and graduated from the University of Belfast. At age 22 or 23 he emigrated to Quebec, where at first he taught school. Shortly afterward, he and his wife Malvina Stone Arthur moved to Burlington, Vermont, where Arthur for a while taught and studied for the bar. A chance attendance at a revival meeting changed his life.

Although he had been a Presbyterian and had married Miss

Stone in an Episcopal ceremony, Arthur now felt "called" to become a Baptist minister. As a general rule Presbyterians and above all Episcopalians have greater social prestige than Baptists, primarily because the former denominations contain far greater proportions of well-to-do and socially prestigious persons in their congregations than do Baptists. The fact remains that some members of each of these Protestant groups are socially uncharacteristic of the rest of their memberships. It therefore follows that adherence to one or another of these churches does not by itself identify the social ranking of an individual or his family. In any case, Arthur became a most successful minister, one whose eloquence attracted overflowing congregations. His income, while superior to that of a working man, did not far exceed $500 per year. It did enable him, however, to devote a portion of his week to the scholarly and literary pursuits that never ceased to fascinate him. He wrote articles for a journal devoted to philosophical, historical, and scientific as well as literary themes. When Chester Arthur was a boy, his father, who spoke Latin, Greek, and Hebrew, was awarded an honorary degree by Union College.

The president's mother was of English descent. She was the granddaughter of Uriah Stone, a prosperous New Hampshire farmer who fought in the Revolution and afterward operated a ferry across the Connecticut River. His seventh son, George Washington Stone, who was Malvina's father, attended Dartmouth College before moving on to Berkshire, Vermont, where he operated a farm. He married Judith Stevens who, according to family tradition, was part Indian, but about whom little else is known.

Stephen Grover Cleveland, the twenty-second—and the twenty-fourth—president, professed indifference to his own genealogy, once saying that he had always been "kept very busy in an attempt to fulfill the duties of life without questioning how I got into the scrape." His best biographer points out that earlier writers had fostered the false impression that Grover Cleveland "rose from a poor and commonplace stock. On the contrary, his forebears were of the truest aristocracy that America can boast; men who . . . made themselves community leaders." The first to come here from England was Moses Cleveland who in 1635 landed in Massachusetts as "an apprentice indentured to a joiner." Subsequently Clevelands almost invariably became Puritan ministers and deacons. Achieving special distinction was the president's great-great-grandfather Aaron, the grandson of the immigrant Moses Cleveland and the son of a businessman and land speculator. Aaron Cleveland graduated from Harvard, became a leader of the Anglican Church and the influential Society for the Propagation of the Gospel in Foreign Parts, and was ultimately ordained an Episcopalian minister. He married into the "aristocratic" Sewell family of Boston. His son, also named Aaron, flourished as a hat manufacturer in Connecticut, where during the Revolution he served in the state legislature. One of his daughters married the wealthy philanthropist, David L. Dodge, founder of the noted commercial family.

Grover Cleveland's father was Richard F. Cleveland, a man who, although he never attained either the wealth or the eminence of the two Aaron Clevelands, was hardly a failure in the ordinary sense of that term. After graduating with honors from Yale, he studied at Princeton Theological Seminary in preparation for the ministry. For a quarter of a century he ministered to congregations, first in Virginia, then in New Jersey and New York, earning local respect, if not broader prestige, before accepting in 1850 the important and influential position of district secretary for the Central New York agency of the American Home Missionary Society. His wife Ann Neal was of a Protestant Anglo-Irish family, the daughter of Abner Neal, a rich publisher and seller of law books.

When Grover Cleveland's father died, the boy went to live with his uncle Lewis F. Allan. Allan was one of the wealthiest and most eminent men in the Buffalo area, a man with his hand in many business activities and a variety of cultural associations. Described as a man who had "money, respect, connections," Allan provided young Cleveland "an atmosphere of refinement" as well as opulence. Cleveland's biographer has a point; it was indeed "something to be [Allan's] nephew."

Benjamin Harrison occupied the presidency between Cleveland's two terms. Harrison's most recent biographer writes that "it would be utterly false to acquiesce in the impression created by campaign biographies" that Harrison descended from "poor but honest stock." For Benjamin Harrison was the grandson of William Henry Harrison. In addition to sharing with his grandfather the Harrison ancestry, the younger man had what the older never did—a grandparent who had been the President of the United States. Had the older man's son John Scott Harrison somehow dissipated the unsurpassed social prestige accumulated by earlier generations of Harrisons? Hardly. If Benjamin's father did not add very much to the family's repute, it was not because of any fall he suffered.

After benefiting from the private tutoring that was characteristic of the education the family provided its young men, John Scott Harrison graduated from college as class valedictorian and began to prepare for the law. He commenced his practice with the prestigious law firm of Longwirth and Harrison, whose senior partner Nicholas Longwirth was a millionaire several times over. The chief reason for John Scott Harrison's slight public achievements was his own father's prominence and pressing public obligations. Since William Henry Harrison was too busy as the chief executive of the United States to look after the family's large and complex estate, his son had to discontinue his own law practice in order to take over what was in effect a full-time responsibility. He nevertheless managed to serve as justice of the peace in his Miami, Ohio, township for twenty years in addition to being appointed to the county board of control that supervised all tax assessments and expenditures, and being elected to Congress. He married Elizabeth Irwin, daughter of Captain Archibald Irwin and granddaughter of James Ramsay, a Scottish gentleman who had come to America, married into the prestigious Agnew family of Philadelphia, and thrived as an importer of flour.

William McKinley was the last president of the nineteenth century. In his reminiscences, McKinley recalled that his childhood days had been "pure luxury." While he appears to have been referring more to the emotional than to the sybaritic pleasures of his youth, McKinley did in fact grow up in a prosperous household. Both his grandfathers fought in the American Revolution.

After the fighting, James McKinley, a Scots-Irishman, headed west from Pennsylvania to become the manager of a charcoal furnace in Ohio. His son, the president's father, also named William McKinley, manufactured pig iron, renting and owning several furnaces on his own and in partnership with his younger brother Benjamin McKinley, and investing too in mining.

If the evidence on the president's paternal side is slim, that on his maternal side is even slimmer, for we know little beyond the fact that his mother Nancy Allison was a Methodist of Scottish descent, whose parents lived in something short of luxury. (Pity that years ago when I was the research assistant to Margaret Leech, as she prepared her Pulitzer prize–winning biography of McKinley, I did not anticipate the theme of this book and try to track down evidence here and abroad on McKinley's ancestry).

The first half of the twentieth century or, in presidential terms, the period from the Republican Roosevelt through his Democratic namesake, witnessed a series of cataclysmic developments. World War I, the fabled prosperity of the 1920s and the Great Depression that followed and was largely caused by the excesses of the twenties, the second world war—these events inevitably affected the American class system, if in ways that even now have not been fully measured. Perhaps most pertinent to the social structure were the progressive income tax made possible by constitutional amendment during Woodrow Wilson's first term and the unprecedentedly large taxes on inherited wealth enacted during the years of Franklin D. Roosevelt's New Deal. The levy on incomes was at first minuscule but, as subsequent events were to show, the fears of its opponents that it would eventually be used more drastically, if not confiscatorily, turned out to be justified. While the first world war temporarily improved the lot of farmers and industrial workers, it more enduringly strengthened the hand of capital. The marvelous living standards that seemed open to all classes during the boom of the twenties turned out to be ephemeral, if not illusory. The depression of the 1930s devastated rural and urban working people at a time when significant governmental assistance to the needy, whether unemployed, ill, or aged, was still a thing of the future.

Some characteristics of upper-class status appear to have been modified in the twentieth century. Activity in local politics or for that matter politics at any level seems to have lost much of its earlier urgency. The nation's magnificent transportation and communications networks had made possible what the sociologist E. Digby Baltzell has called a national upper class. Members of this class would of course live in this or that community, maintaining certain ties there. Increasingly, however, such persons were distinguished by their national, even their international, economic orientation. The economic and material base of upper-class identity shifted from land to finance and industry, and to control of the resources that industry most urgently needed, paralleling the massive change that once and for all shifted the balance of population in America overwhelmingly from rural to urban communities. Nothing in these developments, however, appears to have diminished the gap between the classes or to have equalized the nation's social structure.

In what was unhappily becoming a regular part of the American political tradition, the assassination of a president, in this instance William McKinley, elevated Theodore Roosevelt to the nation's highest office. One of the new president's best biographers describes the Roosevelts as an "upper middle class" family. In view of the actual circumstances and standing of that family, one wonders how the author might have defined *upper* class.

The Roosevelts were a Dutch family, among the earliest settlers of New Amsterdam in the first half of the seventeenth century, who are located by a more recent biographer in the "old New York aristocracy." That is, they possessed the characteristics of patrician families of New York City, Long Island, and Hudson River valley towns nearby: substantial wealth, achieved early, so that later generations could thrive on the interest it accumulated; an exalted social standing featured by exclusiveness and intermarriage with Van Schaicks (later spelled Van Schaack), Astors, and other elite families; a social status so secure that little in the way of public service or renown was needed to maintain it; and a lifestyle the elegance of which transcended mere money.

Not that the Roosevelts lacked means. The president's great-grandfather was a New York City merchant who established a lucrative hardware and glass business in the city's commercial district shortly after the Revolution. His son Cornelius Van Schaick Roosevelt was a fabulously wealthy merchant and banker; by going through all of the city's assessors' notebooks for 1845 in an attempt to discover the location and the value of the properties he owned, I recently discovered that he belonged to the super rich, the wealthiest one-tenth of one percent of the wealthholders in the nation's wealthiest city. His son, the president's father, Theodore Roosevelt, Sr., carried on the family's glass importing business and engaged too in banking. A modern writer speaks of his "moderate wealth." In fact, when C. V. S. Roosevelt died in 1871, he left his son an inheritance of one million dollars. Theodore Roosevelt, Sr., had wealth enough to provide his famous son and his other children all the luxuries of life during their youth—a magnificent home, a corps of servants, an unexcelled private education, expensive and attractive leisure activities such as the Grand Tour of Europe and a journey to Egypt and the Near East one season. The famous house on then fashionable East 20th Street in Manhattan where Theodore, Jr., was born was a gift from C. V. S. Roosevelt, a three-story structure with servants' quarters at the top and a private gym that was built when the president was born. Like most other men of his class, Theodore Roosevelt, Sr., avoided the Civil War by hiring a substitute to fight for him.

He may have been motivated to do so in part out of sensitivity toward his wife's strong pro-Confederate feelings. The president's mother, Martha Bulloch Roosevelt, was descended from a patrician Georgia slaveowning family that had come to Charleston, South Carolina from Scotland, either late in the seventeenth century, as one biographer reports, or early in the eighteenth, as reports another. What is not in question is the great distinction the family achieved, whether in economic, social, or political standing. The pioneer James Bulloch was a classical scholar who became a planter and large landholder, and influential in South Carolina politics. Martha Bulloch's great-grandfather Archibald Bulloch, the first president of Georgia, was the commander in chief of the province when he died in 1776. Her father James Stephen Bulloch was a planter, a banker, a corporate director, and deputy collector of the Port of Savannah. The president's mother was a "magnificent horsewoman," who lived as a child in stately Bulloch Hall with "every advantage" in a setting that has been described as a "wonderland." Coming from the sort of topdrawer Southern aristocratic family that during the antebellum years intrigued the Knickerbocker elite, Martha Bulloch married Theodore Roosevelt, Sr., in Bulloch Hall in 1853.

Guided by the upper-crust ideal of noblesse oblige, Theodore Roosevelt, Sr., threw himself into a great variety of social and humanitarian activities. In addition to joining his fellow swells in the Union League and the Century Association, he helped to establish the Children's Aid Society and was a leading spirit behind the creation of a permanent lodging house for newsboys, an orthopedic hospital, the Young Men's Christian Association, and both the Metropolitan Museum of Art and the American Museum of Natural History. Believing, as did others in his class, that energetic participation in politics was "both trivial and absurd," he turned his back on the prospect of political office. But during the Civil War he served with enthusiasm on the Allotment Commission that was charged with persuading enlisted men to send at least part of their pay to their dependents—a form of high-minded paternalism that his famous son might have described as "bully."

The man Roosevelt chose as his successor was also born to an elite family, if not an extremely wealthy family. William Howard Taft was descended of what earlier writers called eminent New England stock. The American founder was Robert Taft, who settled in Braintree in 1678. He acquired property and served on the town board of selectmen. His son Joseph added to the estate and was a captain in the militia. His wife Elizabeth Emerson Taft was related to the family of Ralph Waldo Emerson. A grandson, Aaron Taft, who was the president's great-grandfather, attended Princeton University and subsequently left the Bay State for Townshend in Windham County, Vermont. His son Peter Rawson Taft was a lawyer as well as a landowner, and won eminence in the state as a judge of the probate and county courts. The son of Peter Rawson and Sylvia Howard Taft was Alphonso Taft, the father of William Howard Taft.

Alphonso Taft achieved perhaps greater distinction than had any of his forebears, earning a reputation as "the first citizen of Cincinnati." Upon graduating from Amherst Academy and Yale, he went into law. A shrewd investor as well as a prominent attorney, at one point in his career he turned down a nomination to a well-paying judgeship on the Superior Court of Cincinnati because it did not match his private income. His service, like his standing, extended well beyond his local community. In addition to sitting on the Superior Court of Ohio, he became the Secretary of War, the Attorney General of the United States, and an ambassador first at Vienna and later at St. Petersburg. William H. Taft grew up in the magnificent brick and stucco Taft mansion, a dwelling surrounded by large grounds, impressive walls, and manicured lawns, in Mount Auburn, Cincinnati. He and his brother received an inheritance of $100,000 from the very wealthy father of Fanny Phelps Taft, Alphonso Taft's first wife. After her death, Taft, who was evidently a most methodical man, visited New England expressly to find a wife and he found her in Louisa Maria Torrey, a woman very much younger than he. The future president's mother came of a distinguished Massachusetts family. Her father Samuel Davenport Torrey was a rich Boston merchant who had retired early on the profits from overseas commerce and who owned the land on which young William Howard Taft spent his summer vacations.

In 1913 the twenty-eighth president, Woodrow Wilson, entered the White House. The new president's grandfather James Wilson was a Scots-Irishman who emigrated from northern Ireland to Philadelphia in 1807 and the following year married Anne Adams, who had come over on the same ship. As little is known of her family as is known of the Wilsons when they lived near Londonderry. James Wilson became well known, however, as he carved out an enviable career in America. After taking over the publication of one of the country's oldest and best-known journals, the Philadelphia *Aurora,* he moved on to Ohio, where he speculated in real estate, became a railroad magnate and a bank director, and played a prominent part in politics. After being elected to the state legislature, he became an associate judge of the court of common pleas, despite the fact that he was not a lawyer. In his later years he was known as Judge Wilson and looked up to as one of the most distinguished men in the state. Of his seven sons, one became a successful publisher in Pittsburgh, two were generals in the Civil War, and another became the adjutant general of Pennsylvania. His son Joseph Ruggles Wilson, Woodrow Wilson's father, was encouraged to become a scholar.

After compiling a brilliant record at Jefferson (later Washington and Jefferson) College, where he was valedictorian, Joseph Wilson earned a B.D. degree at Princeton University, in preparation for the ministry. He taught for a few years, first at Jefferson and then at Hampden-Sidney. In 1855, a year before the future president's birth, he launched what was to be a most distinguished career in the ministry by becoming the pastor of the First Presbyterian Church in Staunton, Virginia. When in 1857 he became the minister of the First Presbyterian Church of Augusta, Georgia, Joseph Wilson was regarded as a "marked man, a leader," the peer of "senators and generals and judges." If he was hardly a rich man, he nevertheless kept his family in unusually "comfortable circumstances," providing young Tommy (Woodrow Wilson was born Thomas Woodrow Wilson) an ample brick house with stables and gardens. His wife Jessie Woodrow Wilson was an heiress to "a considerable sum of money" left by her brother. Her father was one of the leading Presbyterian ministers in Ohio. A modern scholar describes the family (the Wodrows in Scotland, the family's land of origin) as "a more distinguished stock" than the Wilsons. One branch of Woodrow Wilson's mother's family has been traced back to the great Robert Bruce.

During the childhood of Wilson's successor, Warren Gamaliel Harding, his mother Phoebe Elizabeth Dickerson Harding was many times overheard to say she hoped her son would grow up to become the president of the United States. Nothing in the background of the Dickersons suggested that her wish was anything but the expression of faith that was doubtless uttered by countless other American parents. But the president's paternal line was not without distinction. The family dated back in this country to 1623 when the English Puritan Richard Harding came to Braintree, Massachusetts. His grandson Stephen Harding was a successful sea captain and shipbuilder, whose son Abraham became one of the most prosperous farmers and leading citizens in Orange County, New York, where he served as a lieutenant in the Continental army during the Revolution and afterwards as a major in the state militia. His son Abraham Harding, Jr., moved to Wyoming Valley, Pennsylvania, where he "quickly emerged as a man of standing." His son Amos was one of the two largest taxpayers in the village of Clifford that he himself founded. The Hardings soon moved to Ohio, where George Tryon Harding, the president's grandfather, built the largest and most substantial house in the community.

According to Warren Harding's most recent and most thorough biographer, the Harding gravestones in Blooming Grove, Ohio, give "evidence of a family that has made its mark" and become the most prominent family in the area. Warren's father, the second George Tryon Harding, may indeed have lacked the "solid quality" that had made his ancestors leaders in their communities. And yet, as a college graduate, Civil War veteran, farmer, businessman, and doctor, he was hardly a total failure. What has been called "the shadow of Blooming Grove" concerned not any lack of achievement on his part but a rumor of Negro blood in the Harding ancestry, "that would never quite die down." As for the president's mother, she was a midwife. It was only when Warren was a grown man that she began to call herself a doctor and was accepted as such. After she was awarded a license in 1896 she referred to herself as "a specialist in obstetrics and children's diseases." The tawdriness surrounding Warren Harding's behavior in the White House does not and should not be permitted to detract from the standing earned by his family.

Harding's presidency was cut short by his sudden death. Calvin Coolidge now ascended to the high office. The new president was of course a very different personality, a man of far less flamboyance and far more personal integrity than his predecessor. The family status of the one, however, was not very much unlike that of the other. Coolidge's ancestry in this country dates back to 1630 when John Coolidge, an English Puritan, settled in Watertown, Massachusetts. The future president was christened John but he dispensed with the name after he was twenty to avoid confusion, for his father too was named John. The president described the Coolidges as a family of "substance and prominence" for five generations. A modern biographer, while noting that other branches of the family attained prominence as historians, academicians, architects, and diplomats, finds that the president's branch, which relocated in Vermont, were "mavericks," who achieved little beyond modest respect. Yet, the president's memoirs and other evidence indicate that the Vermont Coolidges did better than that.

One ancestor, John Coolidge, was a man of substantial means who had been a captain in the Revolutionary army and was after the war elected and reelected to local office. Calvin Coolidge described his father as, on the one hand, a mason and carriage maker, "very skilled with his hands," and, on the other, as a man constantly sought out by his neighbors to serve and represent them, whether as notary public, justice of the peace, constable, sheriff, or member of the lower house and senate of the state legislature. According to William Allen White, the president's father was the village squire, in addition to being "a merchant prince" and a bank director. In view of John Coolidge's known income and savings and the modest scope of his commercial operations, "merchant prince" seems somewhat an exaggeration. Yet the $1500 in profits he earned each year and his savings of $25,000 placed him much nearer the top than the bottom rung of the nation's wealth ladder. The family of the president's mother, Victoria Josephine Moor Coolidge, were New Englanders of Scottish, Welsh, and English descent, whose social standing was said to equal that of the Coolidges.

Not choosing to run for reelection, Calvin Coolidge left the way open to Herbert Clark Hoover. Hoover was a descendant of

Andreas Huber who, when he was a young boy, came in 1738 to Pennsylvania from the German Palatinate, where the Hubers had fled to escape religious persecution in Switzerland. The family moved west, first to Ohio, then to Iowa. The president's father Jesse Clark Hoover owned a blacksmith shop and a farm implement agency, which he acquired during his son's infancy. He evidently prospered. When he died he was described in the local newspaper's obituary notice as a valuable citizen who would be "sadly missed in business circles." (This allusion appears to be the sole basis of a recent biographer's statement that Jesse Hoover had "high standing" in the business community.) His wife Huldah Minthorn Hoover was born in Ontario to a family that for many generations was prominent in New England.

Herbert Hoover was left an orphan in his youth, his father dying when the boy was six, his mother when he was eight. After living for two years on the farm of an uncle in West Branch, Iowa, young Hoover went to Oregon, to be brought up by his mother's brother, Dr. Henry John Minthorn. Since his own son had recently died, Minthorn became like a father to young Hoover. Dr. Minthorn was a Civil War veteran who was active in his local church and the head of the Friends Pacific Academy that later became Pacific University. In the home of this eminent man Herbert Hoover received and learned the value of a good education.

In the depths of the greatest depression in the nation's history, Franklin Delano Roosevelt was elected president. The Democratic Roosevelt shared two seventeenth-century ancestors with his cousin Theodore and a family status that was at least as dazzling. On his father's side Franklin's branch of the Roosevelt family could be traced back to generations of large landholdings, commercial wealth, and social distinction achieved in part through elite intermarriages. FDR's great-great-grandfather Isaac Roosevelt was a wealthy sugar refiner and merchant who, during the American Revolution, helped draft the first New York State Constitution. His son James added banking to his business activities, married into the prestigious Hoffman family, bred horses, and began to lead the life of a country gentleman on his Hudson River estate. Although James Roosevelt's son, the president's grandfather, earned a medical degree, he never practiced, turning his back on a professional and public life so that he could devote himself to such leisurely pursuits as botany and the breeding of cattle and trotting horses. In the family tradition of social endogamy he married an Aspinwall. The child of this union, also named James, was Franklin's father. This country squire has recently been described as "by profession a retired capitalist." Inheriting an ample landed estate, he invested heavily and profitably in coal lands and railroad securities, the better to secure the elegant life he enjoyed. His sole political involvements came first in 1886 when, as a reward for his lavish financial support to the Cleveland campaign two years earlier, he was named first secretary to the American legation in Vienna, and again in 1895 when he was named to a similar post in London. The estate he left his son was, at less than half a million dollars, not a lavish one but it was ample, particularly when supplemented by the valuable stamp collection FDR inherited from his mother. The youth enjoyed by the future president, marked by private tutors, European trips, and the elegance and comfort of the family's magnificent home in Hyde Park, was one that millions upon millions more could hardly have improved.

James Roosevelt first married Rebecca Howland of the great northeastern maritime and merchant family. His second wife, Franklin's mother Sara Delano Roosevelt, came of a family that, in the language of a biographer, "could recite pedigrees from a repertoire that seemed to include half the aristocracy of Europe and all that of the Hudson River Valley. At least a dozen lines of *Mayflower* descent converged in Franklin and Sara could name every one of them." Her father Warren Delano had made a fortune, first in the China trade and later in coals and minerals. He left his daughter a financial legacy of one million dollars and a social legacy that more money than that could not buy. She evidently believed that political office, even the highest, was a comedown for her son.

Roosevelt's death just before the end of World War II elevated Harry S. Truman to the highest office. In his memoirs Truman calls attention to the fact that John Tyler's brother was the father of his grandmother and "the whole Tyler family is mixed up with both sides" of his father's family. Harry Truman's great-grandfather William Truman was a successful farmer who owned land and slaves and left a sizeable inheritance to his son Anderson Shippe Truman. The president's grandfather held the office of director of schools for a number of years in his Kentucky community. It was his son John, Harry Truman's father, who moved the family to Independence, Missouri.

John Truman farmed and dealt in livestock. When he was a boy the president lived in a "big house," maintained by the $15,000 that his parents averaged in good years. The president's mother Martha Ellen Young Truman came of a family that ranked higher socially than the Trumans. Her father Solomon Young was an astute landowner and businessman who, after receiving a modest inheritance of several thousand dollars, increased it more than a hundredfold. He left Martha Ellen and her brother a farm worth $150,000. His wife Harriet Louisa Gregg, Harry Truman's maternal grandmother, came of a family of "some means" and standing.

☆☆☆

If historical developments since the end of the second world war are particularly hard to put in perspective because they are so close to us, they have also been the most intensively examined by students of social structure. The continuing revolution in technology in the age of automation and the computer has led some thinkers to the conclusion that the social as well as the occupational structure must inevitably be transformed and that, as a matter of fact, the transformation is ostensibly well under way. Daniel Bell is not the only scholar who speaks of a "post-industrial age" in which old occupational categories are said to be cast aside, industrialism drastically altered, if not supplanted, and power transferred from traditional sources of wealth to the new men of science and learning who can best command the amazing computerized technology of the new time. At the moment some of these developments are more conjectural than real. True, working people in greater numbers wear white rather than blue collar. Yet to judge from the evidence gathered in the dozens of examinations of wealth, income, distribution of community power, and related themes, stratification in American society does not appear to have diminished in the post–World War II years, for all the brave talk to the contrary.

Smoldering dissatisfaction with foreign policy and internal developments in American life resulted, during the years of the Korean and Vietnam wars, in the outbreak of civil rights, women's rights, and young people's "revolutions." While these movements did accomplish some important changes, they were revolutions only in a rhetorical sense. For not only did they settle for changes within the system; there are no signs that they significantly affected the distribution of wealth, status, or power within the American social hierarchy.

The hero of the nation's most recent great war seems to have an inside track to the presidency—so long as that war is perceived by the people as legitimate or authentic. (Why the nation chose Harding and "normalcy" after World War I is, I fear, too complex a story to be told here.) The Revolutionary War produced George Washington, the War of 1812 Andrew Jackson, the Mexican War Zachary Taylor, the Civil War Ulysses S. Grant, the Spanish-American War Theodore Roosevelt, and World War II Dwight David Eisenhower.

☆ ☆ ☆

A family legend has it that Eisenhowers had been "mounted and armed warriors in a medieval German army." Alas, evidence is lacking to sustain this romantic fancy. Three Eisenhower brothers appear to have migrated to Pennsylvania in the early eighteenth century. Dwight David Eisenhower's great-grandfather Frederick evidently prospered as a weaver and added to his property by marrying Barbara Ann Miller. She was a blood tie of the famous general Winfield Scott and she brought to the marriage a "very generous dowry." Their son Jacob, Ike's grandfather, was an admired minister who bought and farmed an expensive property in Pennsylvania before selling it for a large profit and moving to Kansas. He thrived in that state both as a farmer and as a minister in the Church of the Brethren in Christ. His daughter Amanda married C. O. Musser, who made a small fortune out of a large creamery. His son, David, the future president's father, did not fare so well, certainly not financially. One biographer claims that Dwight Eisenhower's parents lived on the wrong side of the tracks in their home town, Abilene, where ostensibly they were "common people, poor people."

Actually, David had received from his father a marriage gift of a 160-acre farm and $2,000 in cash—a gift that was beyond the dreams of the great majority of the people of the time, the 1880s. Unfortunately, David put this money into a general merchandise store that failed dismally. Eventually he went to work in the Musser creamery, earning between $100 and $200 a month as an engineer. During Ike's boyhood, his father bought an "imposing house" from a relative and the family did well. Of Ida Elizabeth Stover, David's wife, we know very little, other than that she was one of eleven children and came of a family that had migrated to America in the 1730s. Its subsequent history has been called "remarkably similar" to that of the Eisenhowers. As a young woman Ida Elizabeth Stover attended Lane College on her small inheritance, certainly a rare activity for a young woman in that time.

In 1960 the nation selected its first Catholic president, John Fitzgerald Kennedy. The Kennedys achieved dazzling financial heights, and lofty, if not quite as brilliant, social status, but they did so within an Irish Catholic community that in John F. Kennedy's youth was still regarded as socially inferior by many among the Protestant elite. The success was hard-earned and recent, traceable only two generations back to the president's grandparents. His great-grandfather Patrick Kennedy was a tenant farmer, but one whose small holding in southeast Ireland evidently compared favorably with the tiny parcels worked by most families in the impoverished southwest. He managed by 1848 to accumulate the "small fortune" necessary to pay for his passage to Boston. He was working as a cooper when he died at age 35 of cholera.

His son Patrick Joseph Kennedy began work as a stevedore. He used his savings to open a saloon in East Boston which did extremely well. Before long Kennedy had expanded into retail and wholesale whiskey distribution, played an important part in the organization of several banks, and become a leader in the Boston Irish community. He was elected to the state house of representatives in 1886 and six years later to the senate. He married Mary Hickey, whose family "stood a rung or two above the Kennedys." His son, the president's father, Joseph Patrick Kennedy, was born into an affluent and locally prominent family that lived in an attractive four-story house situated on a hill overlooking the harbor. Joseph Kennedy attended the exclusive Boston Latin School, "where the sons of New England's leading families had been educated since 1635," before enrolling at Harvard. At the time of John's birth, Joseph Kennedy was an assistant manager in the Bethlehem shipyards in Quincy, earning $20,000 a year. A bank president at age 25, a successful businessman, and a movie producer who in the 1920s earned $6,000 a week playing the market, Joseph during his son's youth proceeded to amass a large part of the huge fortune that enabled him to bring up his children in upper-class comfort, with servants, nurses, governesses, and other trappings of wealth.

His marriage to Rose Fitzgerald significantly abetted the upward climb of Joseph Patrick Kennedy financially and, above all, socially. For in view of her father John Fitzgerald's prominence and his own clear appreciation of it, "Honey Fitz" at first did not regard Kennedy as a suitable match for a young woman of "high Irish family," such as his daughter. Fitzgerald, who had been a congressman before becoming mayor of Boston, was used to moving in lofty circles not inhabited by Irish Catholics alone. Rose was the "belle of Irish Boston" at the time she made her debut at a "glittering party," following a genteel and exclusive education in this country and abroad. Before her betrothal to Joseph Kennedy, rumor had it that she would marry her father's friend, the fabulously wealthy yachtsman Sir Thomas Lipton.

The assassination of Kennedy vaulted Lyndon Baines Johnson into the White House. The standing of Lyndon Johnson's parents and grandparents is difficult to determine, in part because it seemed to fluctuate wildly and in part because much of what earlier commentators thought they knew about the matter had been told them by Johnson himself. According to his most thorough biographer, Johnson enlisted "all his energy and all his cunning" in a "lifelong attempt to obscure, not only the true facts of his rise to power . . . but even of his youth"; "most of the stories [he told about his early years] were false."

The evidence on Lyndon Johnson's parents and grandparents must be treated warily. Johnson's confidante Doris Kearns reports that LBJ liked to assume "the posture of a Horatio Alger figure who rose from rags to riches by hard work, determination, pluck and luck." Johnson indeed displayed such traits and he enjoyed too the necessary good fortune. But he did not start precisely from rags. On his maternal side, one of his ancestors had been on the staff of Col. Francis Marion, the famous "swamp fox" of the American Revolution. LBJ's great-great-grandmother was the sister of a Kentucky governor and of congressmen from that state and from Tennessee. His great-grandfather Robert Holmes Bunton was a well-to-do cattleman, rancher, and planter. This man's daughter Eliza Bunton married Sam Ealy Johnson, the grandfather of the future president. A Confederate army veteran, Sam Johnson began to accumulate cattle during the Civil War and after the war joined his brother Tom as one of the largest cattle drivers in the counties west of San Antonio. The brothers had one hundred cowboys working for them and in 1870 they earned $100,000 from the sale of a herd of 7,000 cattle they drove up to Kansas. In other years they owned between four and five times that number. But Sam Johnson's fortune ran through his fingers after the financial panic of 1873 and the drought that destroyed the cattle industry. Robert Caro writes that in 1880, when Sam and Eliza Johnson moved back to the Pedernales, they were poor and during the next thirty years "grew poorer." Interestingly, however, Sam had much popular support when he ran, unsuccessfully, for a seat in the state legislature in 1892, losing out to his son-in-law.

LBJ's father, also Sam Johnson, had a strikingly checkered career. LBJ was not engaging in hyperbole when he later said of his childhood and youth: "One year we'd all be riding high in Pedernales terms, so high in fact that on a scale of A to F, we'd be right up there with the A's. Then two years later, he'd lose it all. The cotton he had bought for 44 cents a bale had dropped to the bottom of the heap." His father's economic circumstances were indeed kaleidoscopic.

A schoolteacher at age 19, Sam Johnson, Jr., subsequently rented his father's farm, which he operated with the assistance of several hired hands. During his good years he traded in cotton futures, made money in real estate, and moved the family into "a snug, three-bedroom white frame house" in Johnson City. When LBJ was young, his father bought a new Hudson car and hired a chauffeur to drive it, after netting $17,000 in one real estate deal. At the height of his success, Sam Johnson, Jr., bought a newspaper, ranches, a small auditorium, and Johnson City's only hotel, among other properties. He was considered the leading man in the community in 1918, the year when the governor of Texas visited and ate at the Johnson's house. For Sam Johnson was prominent in politics as well as successful in business. After serving one term as justice of the peace in 1902, he was two years later elected to the first of his many terms in the state legislature. A legislator's pay of $300 a year permitted no man to grow rich from membership in the body; since it met for only sixty days, every other year, no one was expected to abandon his job or enterprises, whatever they might be. Election was, nevertheless, an honor, and particularly so when, as happened to Sam Johnson in 1918, a man ran unopposed. Having fallen several thousand dollars in debt in 1906, two years before his famous son was born, Sam Johnson, Jr., made a comeback almost immediately after, assuring the future president a comfortable and comparatively privileged youth. There was, however, to be no comeback after a ruinous drop in cotton prices drove the family deep into a debt from which it never emerged during Sam Johnson's lifetime. His downfall does not detract from the earlier success enjoyed by Lyndon Johnson's father during the first thirteen years of his son's life.

By the standards of the time, Sam Johnson, Jr., married upward when he married Rebekah Baines, for her family were more genteel, far better educated, and commanded much higher social status than the Johnsons. A Baylor University graduate who was one of the few Texas women of her time to complete a higher education, Rebekah was the granddaughter of George Washington Baines, the founder of Baylor University. He was also a theologian, a leader of the Baptist Church, a onetime member of the Arkansas state legislature, all in all a "paragon" of his community. His son, Rebekah's father Joseph Wilson Baines, suffered financial disaster late in life but earlier he had been eminently successful as teacher, lawyer, pillar of the church, secretary of the state of Texas, as well as state legislator and newspaper owner. Reduced to writing political dispatches for a Galveston newspaper, Joseph Baines one day sent his daughter to interview a well-thought-of young Texas representative, Sam Johnson, Jr., for his newspaper. Rebekah Baines brought home more than a story.

Biographers differ about the standing of the family of Lyndon Johnson's successor. In 1729, Thomas Milhous, a Quaker from County Kildare, Ireland, came to Chester County, Pennsylvania, preceding by a quarter of a century the arrival of the first Nixon in Delaware, also from Ireland. Contrasting appraisals of what followed have been offered. One reports that a Nixon crossed the Delaware with George Washington, that another died at Gettysburg, and that the line is sprinkled with preachers, teachers, and merchants, some of whom attained local prominence. Another writer, accentuating the negative, observes that for all their headstart in America, the Nixons and Milhouses accomplished little, rarely advancing beyond the status of poor, illiterate or semiliterate dirt farmers. Where is truth?

Certainly neither family achieved true eminence. Richard Nixon's grandfather Samuel Brady Nixon failed as a small farmer, scratching out a living as a mail carrier and teacher. His son Francis Anthony Nixon was the father of the future president. Unlike his younger brother, who went on to earn a Ph.D. degree and become an agricultural expert, Frank Nixon quit school early, after no more than six years of formal education. Described as a "rolling stone," Frank Nixon wandered from Ohio to California, working as a house painter, telephone lineman, trolley car motorman, carpenter, glass worker, and sheep rancher, among other jobs. As was the case with so many presidents' fathers, he married upward socially, taking as his wife Hannah Milhous, whose family was both more stable and more prosperous than his own. Although Richard Nixon was born in a house in Yorba Linda that was hard to keep warm in very cold weather, by the time he was ten years old his father's combination gas station and general store was doing well and the family had earned a position of respect in their California Quaker community.

Nixon's unprecedented resignation raised a vice-president suddenly to the presidency for the ninth time in the nation's history. Gerald R. Ford was born Leslie Lynch King, the son of Leslie King, a wool dealer, and Dorothy Gardner King. When the marriage ended two years later in divorce, Dorothy Gardner returned to her family in Grand Rapids where shortly afterward she married Gerald R. Ford. The future president was now formally adopted by his stepfather and renamed Gerald R. Ford, Jr.

The Fords and Gardners were both descended of early English settlers who, after the break with the mother country, became members of the Episcopalian Church. Gerald R. Ford, Sr., owned a paint business that began to flourish shortly after his marriage. The family moved to a large three-story house in the fashionable part of town and regularly took long and expensive vacations in Florida. A childhood friend later remembered Gerald Ford, Jr., as a rich boy. A biographer concludes that if the president's stepfather was "never really a man of wealth" in the full sense of the term, he was prosperous enough to maintain his family in solid comfort. In addition to being a successful businessman, the elder Ford was active in the Grace Episcopal Church, the Boy Scouts, and a variety of Grand Rapids civic organizations. In the kind of small but vital industrial city that by early in the twentieth century had become the nation's most characteristic milieu, the social ranking of the Fords was quite high.

In 1976 Ford was defeated for reelection by the little-known James Earl Carter. According to an amateur genealogist, who is described as a "fifth generation Carter himself," Jimmy Carter is a direct descendant of Alfred the Great of England. Another undocumented story traces the Carters in America to a "Sir Thomas Carter," a wealthy planter who supposedly set foot on the New World in 1650. The president himself observes only that the first of the name to be buried in the family cemetery a few miles north of Plains, Georgia, is Wiley Carter, who died in 1798. An uncle speaks of a Wiley Carter—perhaps the son of the man referred to by the president—who farmed in Georgia during the first half of the nineteenth century, left each of his many children substantial land, and was descended from James Carter of Virginia, a Patriot during the Revolutionary War. In yet another version, Carters, who before the Civil War had been slaveowning cotton farmers and merchants, were afterward peanut farmers "just one notch above the black sharecroppers who worked on their land." What is more certain is that Jimmy Carter was born on land that had been in the family five generations. His paternal grandmother evidently lived in a large house in town.

The president's recollection is that his father Earl Carter was "an extremely competent farmer and businessman who later developed a wide range of interests in public affairs." The positive appraisal of father by son does not appear to be exaggerated. After returning from the first world war, in which he served as an officer, Earl Carter proved an enterprising farmer and businessman who, in his son's words, was extremely intelligent, "well read about current events, and . . . always probing for innovative business techniques and enterprises." He not only probed, he acted. The Carter farm produced a great assortment of crops, meats, and timber products. Earl Carter also invested in machinery for processing cane stalks and making syrup. The farm of this enterprising man contained its own tennis court. According to the president's mother, Earl Carter left a "considerable sum of money," when he died.

When Jimmy Carter was a boy, his father was a director of the Rural Electification Program in Plains. He was active too in the Plains Baptist Church, he sat on the county school board, and he was elected to the state legislature. *Why Not the Best?* appears to be accurate in describing Earl Carter as a "natural leader in the Plains community." In common with most other reporters of presidential ancestries, the president tells little about his mother or her family, the Gordys, other than that she sometimes doubled as a registered nurse and community doctor, in addition to performing "the natural functions of a mother and a housekeeper." The world of Plains was a tiny one of slightly more than five hundred people during the president's youth. The Carters occupied a high place in that world.

In 1980 the nation elected to the presidency Ronald Wilson Reagan, erstwhile sportscaster, Hollywood actor, business spokesman, television personality, and governor of California. Little is known of the president's family other than the slight and not very informative references he made to it in the autobiography he wrote in 1965. Offering no information whatever on his grandparents on either the paternal or maternal side, the president's account devotes a few scant paragraphs to his circumstances at birth, not much more attention to his father's various jobs and the lifestyle they made possible, and typically, next to nothing about the family of his mother, Nell Wilson Reagan.

The evidence has been variously interpreted. Looking back on his infancy and youth, Reagan has observed that "we were poor, but I didn't know it at the time." In the classic tradition of successful men poor-mouthing and therefore romanticizing their youth, Reagan said, "Our family didn't exactly come from the wrong side of the tracks, but were certainly within sound of the train whistles." He observed that during his youth, his father had only once bought a new car and the family had never lived in a house they owned. In a news conference in June, 1983 he asked how he could be charged with lack of sympathy for the poor when his own youth was marked by poverty. And yet the president's own evidence has led one of his few biographers to describe Reagan's as "a picture-book boyhood . . . out of an old Norman Rockwell cover for the *Saturday Evening Post*," a youth typically marked by good times, attractive housing, and solid middle-class comforts.

According to the president's version, his father John Edward Reagan was a "first generation black Irishman," an Irish Catholic who conformed to one element of the popular stereotype by drinking to excess but confounded another by his righteous aversion to anti-Semitism and white racism. This was evidently a most serious man who, since "he loved shoes," spent many hours "analyzing the bones of the foot." He was a shoe salesman.

The future president was born in a five-room apartment above the general store in Tampico, Illinois, where his father worked. From the time of Ronald Reagan's birth until he was nine, his family "lived in a succession of small towns west of Chicago, as well as in the city itself," as his father, spurred on by restlessness and ambition, sought and found "excellent jobs," whether as salesman on a drawing account, general store manager, or partner in a shoe and boot shop. Reagan points out that his father never earned more than fifty-five dollars a week. But that sum was evidently enough to enable the family to live in attractive rented houses on tree-lined streets in scenic areas. From the time Ronald Reagan was nine until he completed college the family lived in Dixon, Illinois, where the elder Reagan attained his "economic high-water mark." Shortly after Ronald Reagan's graduation, his father was placed in charge of the WPA program in Dixon. Government programs to help the poor are not normally directed by men themselves poor.

The president's mother was a "Scots-English" Protestant who, like her husband, "never graduated from any school but the elementary grades." Without reflecting on their possible social implications, the president attributes to her a variety of social involvements and humanitarian activities, such as performing "regular readings for the various ladies' societies" and visiting and comforting local indigents and jail inmates. According to the sociologists and social historians who specialize in these matters, such benevolence has usually been confined to women of the comfortably situated social classes.

Such were the social origins of the presidents. It remains to be seen how their early circumstances compared with the circumstances of most American families. The chapter that follows undertakes such a comparison. It should already be clear from the evidence presented in this chapter, however, that the families of the presidents were remarkably successful for the most part, typical only if they came from a society that was overwhelmingly populated by people who were successful in material accumulation and highly regarded socially. An enduring myth has contended that American society has always been precisely so arranged. The next chapter reports the extent to which these dual myths of near universal American prosperity and the social and economic representativeness of the nation's most exalted political leaders are borne out by the historical evidence.

☆☆☆☆☆ CHAPTER THREE ☆☆☆☆☆

The Families of the Presidents and the People Compared

THE EVIDENCE PRESENTED in the previous chapter refutes the popular assumption that most presidents were born into families of humble or modest rank and condition. For all its richness and abundance, however, the evidence on the presidents' parents, grandparents, and relatives does not by itself indicate how typical the presidents' youthful circumstances were. Conceivably most people have been similarly well off. In order to find out how representative the families of a small group of leaders are, it is necessary to gather evidence on the people they led. Fortunately such evidence exists. While inevitably it is not nearly as substantial as the evidence on the families of the golden thirty-nine who came to occupy the White House, it is sufficient to afford a clear-cut answer to the question: How do the social standing and material circumstances of the presidents' families compare with the standing and circumstances of the American people as a whole?

Making such a comparison requires us to place each of the presidential families in its appropriate level in the American social structure, to estimate the proportions or percentages of American families to be placed on these levels, and then to compare the percentages of presidential and rank-and-file families located in the high, low, and middle ranks. In other words, the families of the presidents and the people must be assigned to one or another social class.

The idea that classes and class barriers exist in American society appears to be uncongenial to most Americans—at least as unpopular as is the suggestion that our highest leaders typically were born with silver spoons in their mouths. For, as Woodrow Wilson once observed, Americans like to think that "this is the country where there is . . . no distinction of class, . . . no distinction of social status." Numerous surveys and questionnaires conducted by sociologists in the two generations since Wilson spoke show that our attitudes have not changed very much. Americans continue to insist that there are no classes here or claim that they and almost everyone else belong to the great middle class. And now as earlier we continue to subscribe to Alexis de Tocqueville's dictum of almost one hundred and fifty years ago that class is insignificant in America in view of how easily class barriers are brushed aside and how regularly fortunes are won, lost, and won again in what we like to think is this fluid and kaleidoscopic social milieu.

These are no doubt comforting beliefs but, alas, they do not seem to be true. Modern sociologists and social historians have performed many dozens of studies revealing that throughout our history the American people, no less than people abroad, have lived in a society in which families have strikingly dissimilar shares of material goods, social repute, and community influence. In short, they belong to different classes. And far from being a matter of indifference, class is of vital importance to people, shaping almost every aspect of their lives. Nor do they easily ascend from the lower levels to the higher. Movement up the social ladder has always been much rarer in real life than it is in popular myth.

The fact that class in America is, for all its importance, an informal, imprecise, and ever-changing phenomenon no doubt explains why many people are either unaware of it or underestimate its significance. Neither government nor any other institution advises people of the class they belong to. Nor is a fixed and authoritative meaning given to class; there seem to be almost as many definitions as there have been scholars offering them. That is why whoever speaks of class must make clear what he means by the term.

In my usage, a family's class—and I agree with the many sociologists who regard the family, not the individual, as the atomic unit of class—is determined by a combination or blending of the following elements: its comparative wealth and possessions; its income and the prestige of how it is earned; its lifestyle, which includes its uses of leisure and the quality of education it can afford for its young; its prestige, repute, status, or standing, which depends in part on the social circle it moves in and on how far back the family can be traced in the community; and its influence and power. (The last two elements are not the same thing. As Prince Charles recently observed, he may have much influence but he has little or no power.)

This is by no means a perfect definition. But of course there can be no perfect definition that enables us accurately to fix the class standing of families and individuals. The intangible criteria of class such as status and influence cannot be precisely measured and the necessity to make subjective rankings, even of such tangible criteria as occupation or neighborhood, assure the impossibility of creating an objective or universally approved system for assigning people to a particular class. It is enough that a definition be sensible and that it correspond, as I believe my definition does, to long-accepted usage by informed people. The problem with the famous Marxist definition—which stresses two classes, capitalists and workers, each having a distinctive relationship to the means of production, and which emphasizes, too, class consciousness—is that it does not seem to capture the complex American reality. Two or even three classes, if one adds the middle, seem an insufficient number. For much of American history capitalists are better described as the men who controlled the commerce in goods produced than as those who controlled the means of production. Classes here have each contained families with unlike relationships to the means of production. And the "consciousness" of Americans has provided a most misleading clue to their actual positions in the class structure. It has too often been "false consciousness," to use a term that Marxists reserve for another purpose but that appears to be apt in this context.

Before proceeding to describe the classes that constitute the American social structure and estimating the proportions of presidential families and families in the general population that are located within these classes, I think it necessary first to explain both the artificiality and the usefulness of such an exercise.

There is not now and there has never been in the past an American social or class structure. The term is merely a figure of speech, no more a reality than is the "textbook manor" that medievalists are fond of talking about. Throughout its history the United States has had not a single class structure but a variety of dissimilar class structures. Communities of different age, size, population, geographical location, wealth, level of economic development, and historical experiences are likely to have somewhat dissimilar class structures at any moment in time. Whether in Thomas Jefferson's time or Lyndon Johnson's, isolated rural communities do not have the same social order as thriving seaboard cities. And the class structure of all communities changes over the course of time, as the histories of places like Charleston, South Carolina, Davidson County, Tennessee, or Genessee County, New York, make clear. What we call the American class structure, then, is an averaging-out of a great number of diverse and constantly changing structures. It is a fiction but a useful fiction, precisely as is the textbook manor, which although unlike any manor that ever existed is sufficiently like all of them to enable us better to understand all manors by its representation of their important common characteristics.

The chief justifications for speaking of a single American class structure are the large degree of similarity among the class structures of different communities at any given time and the extent of continuity, particularly in the gulfs between the classes, despite all the changes that have occurred over the course of time. For example, slavery has been extinct for one hundred and twenty years, indentured servitude for longer than that. Yet even if the precise occupational, social, and legal status of those who make up the lower classes in America has changed, lower classes remain with us. The upper crust in Benjamin Franklin's Philadelphia accumulated their wealth by, and owed their prestige to, different social roles than those of their modern counterparts but old elite and new, alike, are numerically minuscule groups occupying the highest social plateau of their eras.

The social or class structure, whether of a single community or of the society as a whole, is a metaphysical *vertical* scale that places families at one or another level with other families similarly situated, with those commanding the most attractive and enviable circumstances at the top (nearest heaven?), the most forlorn groups at the bottom, and all others in between. There is of course no fixed number of these classes. Simplifiers speak of two or three classes; the finicky can create literally dozens of classes in their concern that the subtlest nuances of difference in material or social situation of different individuals and families be faithfully categorized. I think there is much to recommend the six-level or six-class American social structure that is used by many sociologists. Working down from the top, these are the upper upper followed by the lower upper, the upper middle, the lower middle, the upper lower, and the lower lower classes. These six categories capture well the spiritual entity of prestige or repute that differentiates American families from one another. And the flexibility of these class categories makes them usable across both space and time, in a way that functional or occupational categories could not match. For the latter classifications have varied meanings at any single moment and new meanings at later moments. For example, to speak of "professionals" as a single class overlooks the very drastic dissimilarities between, say, lawyers eking out a living servicing the claims of the poor and solicitors to the corporate mighty. To treat justices of the peace as men who hold an insignificant office that many a Hollywood film (featuring midnight marriages requiring the fellows to be routed out of bed) ridicules does not do justice to the very great prestige justices of the peace had in James Madison's time. In contrast to the internal differentiation and the changing status that make particular occupations or particular political positions inappropriate social indicators, the broad and loose categories "upper upper" or "lower middle" class serve well for any place and any time, since they can absorb within them every manner of economic, social, or political activity, no matter how varied they may be at any one time and despite whatever changes they may have undergone with the passage of time. The rich and prestigious lawyer, in other words, must be placed higher on the social ladder than his ambulance-chasing colleague, the justice of the peace one hundred and seventy-five years ago higher than his modern counterpart.

Let me try to present a succinct and historically valid portrait of each of the six classes. Families in the upper upper class are and have been wealthy enough to live, if they wish, in material splendor. Their income is high and earned in prestigious ways, whether by inheritance, investments, lands, corporate directorships, large-scale industry, commerce overseas and domestic, shipbuilding or other forms of transportation, great success in the professions, or a combination of these. Their fortunes are substantial enough to permit adult family members to devote themselves entirely to nonutilitarian pursuits and diversions. Their riches, the admired means through which they have been accumulated, and their often dazzling and well-publicized lifestyle appear to confer on them vast, if immeasurable, social prestige. Their children attend the nation's most exclusive schools. If their wealth and their positions of command in finance, commerce, land and industry give them great economic power, their dominant roles in the influential voluntary associations that have for two centuries complemented the powers of government and their direct and indirect influence over politics bespeak their great power whether in their local or the larger community.

The main distinction between families in the upper upper and the lower upper class seems to be the longer duration rather than the dimensions of the former's wealth, renown, and influence. Also differentiating the one elite echelon from the other are subtle gradations of social acceptability. American literature offers many instances of relatively nouveau riche members of the lower upper class trying desperately and not always successfully to crack the charmed and exclusive circle inhabited by the upper

upper as they dine, party, vacation, attend elite social clubs, and spend their leisure (pronounced, of course, as in *treasure*) among their own sort.

What scholars call the upper middle class is in most important respects more like the lower upper than the lower middle class. Its members live well, if not opulently, doing so through socially honorific occupations, whether in land, business, the professions, or the arts. If typically they have not accumulated much wealth, they nevertheless enjoy incomes that assure good housing, attractive possessions, and gratifying uses of leisure (pronounced perhaps as in *seizure*). In the twentieth century their children attend college, if not the most exclusive prep schools. If not in the very top positions, upper-middle-class individuals are nevertheless active in influential voluntary associations as well as in politics, and they command the respect and admiration of those below. (Many surveys have shown that the "lower orders" tend to lump together the relatively successful, comfortably situated, well-regarded members of the upper middle class with the families in the upper classes above them. The view from the bottom, where many live at the edge of want, does not make fine distinctions among those immune to such experiences.)

In view of centuries of usage to the contrary, it is doubtless too late to call the upper middle one of the upper classes. But surely, considering the relatively attractive material circumstances of its members, the prestige of their occupations, the opportunities afforded their children, and their active and influential role in community affairs, the upper middle is what might be called one of the *successful* classes.

A great distance below in prestige and influence, if slightly less so in wealth and income, is the lower middle class. Small shopkeepers, clerks, middle-level white collar workers, foremen and skilled industrial workers in urban communities, small farmers of slight property and modest income in rural areas—lower-middle-class families appear neither to suffer what Tocqueville called the "sting of want" nor to enjoy great material comfort. They usually have slight community involvement, repute, and influence over public affairs.

The lower classes are almost totally lacking in property, prestige, and power. And yet there are qualitatively significant if quantitatively slight distinctions between the upper lower and the class below. Adult heads of household in the upper lower are likely to be semiskilled workers in urban milieus or marginal farmers who either lease their lands from others or labor under heavy mortgage debts. If their families lack attractive possessions, homes, amenities, and uses of leisure, and have little margin to fall back on when unemployment or unanticipated disaster strikes, they are nevertheless likely to own or have access to the material necessities. The lower lower class has always included among its more unfortunate components persons who are the American equivalent of a lumpen proletariat. It contains almost all pre–Civil War blacks, slave or free, the unskilled, the nation's amazingly low-paid agricultural workers and tenant farmers, the chronically unemployed and the unemployable. Even in the era of the welfare state its members live below what public agencies describe as a minimally acceptable level.

Such are the social categories or classes that compose the American class structure.

The distinctions between them are very great indeed but they would lose much of their significance if families easily changed their positions, moving freely and regularly, whether up or down the social ladder, as popular mythology and some scholars insist they have. The suggestion is an inspired one but it is not supported by the historical record. Some individuals have of course enjoyed dramatic rises, others have suffered bad falls, and many have made more money, increasing their savings and possessions as they got older. Such "small-distanced" or incremental improvement, however, is not synonymous with movement up the social scale from one class to another. Stability, not discontinuity, has been the characteristic motif of American social history.

The great question of course concerns the percentages or proportions of the American people that belong in each of the six classes. Several modern sociologists (of the sort that Marxist critics call "mainstream") have offered estimates for the mid-twentieth century that average out as follows:

Class	*Percentage of the American Population in Each Class*
Upper Upper	1
Lower Upper	2
Upper Middle	9–10
Lower Middle	32
Upper Lower	34
Lower Lower	21

These figures point to a striking imbalance or what sociologists call a sharply stratified class structure. As the scholars presenting them would have no doubt agreed, these are something less than figures carved in stone. They are subjective estimates. Alter slightly the weight or significance affixed to any of the criteria defining class and the percentage of families assigned to one or another of the classes also changes. And yet a great weight of germane evidence on the late-eighteenth and the nineteenth centuries as well as on the twentieth century indicate that the dramatic disparities represented by these figures do not exaggerate the historical reality. In the absence of any single modern study or series of studies setting forth the necessary information, the following observations draw on *The Historical Statistics of the United States*, my own and other scholars' research, tax assessors' notebooks and census enumerators' manuscript schedules, wills, probate inventories, and other primary sources, as well as scholarly studies bearing on different facets of class for communities in all sections of the United States and for all periods in American history.

During the first century after independence, most American families made their living in agriculture, the proportion diminishing from about four-fifths at the start to two-thirds in the 1840s; it was not until 1880 that it dropped to slightly less than half. The size of farms and the value of land varied greatly, not only between geographical sections and regions but also within a single state. Evidence available for the three decades after 1850 indicates that the mean average of farms was about 175 acres, a figure that is of course larger than the size of most farms, including as it does the acreage of very great landowners. Statistical evidence on farm earnings is meager for before the mid-nineteenth century but what historians call impressionistic or scattered, not necessarily representative, evidence indicates that farm families in the northeast and northwest typically worked very hard for exceedingly long hours to attain a crude sufficiency. Food was ample but possessions simple, and leisure in very short supply; young people could not be spared from full-time work. Adult farm labor during these years earned roughly $10.00 a month. The material circumstances of white as well as black farmers in the South can be gleaned from evidence on the economics of slavery.

From the time of Washington's election to the election of Lincoln, blacks constituted about eighteen percent of the national population. On the eve of the Civil War, blacks, almost ninety percent of whom were slaves, were almost twenty-five percent of the nation's agricultural population. *Time on the Cross,* the provocative recent study of the economics of slavery, has been widely praised by journalists for its importance and originality but sharply condemned by experts in economic history for its errors and misleading data. Yet even if one accepts its authors' arguments that slaves ate comparatively well (well enough to enable them to work very hard indeed), were spurred on by money and other material incentives, and were treated far less harshly than Harriet Beecher Stowe, the author of *Uncle Tom's Cabin,* ever dreamed, slaves and almost all free blacks can be placed no higher than in the lower lower class. Having an average market value of $1,000 each, slaves were valuable property whose ownership throws additional light on the distribution of wealth. Before the Civil War, less than one white Southern family in four owned any slaves at all. The very great disparities between the relatively small number of white families who owned large numbers of slaves and all other white families are expressed most clearly by the following figures for the mid-nineteenth century: only about ten percent of white Southern families owned as many as five slaves; five percent of whites, as many as ten; between two and three percent, as many as twenty; less than one-half of one percent, as many as fifty; and about one-tenth of one percent owned the hundred or more slaves that Andrew Jackson owned on one of his Tennessee plantations alone.

During the past century, as the agricultural population has diminished at an ever-swifter pace, from thirty-five percent of the whole in 1900 to twelve percent in 1950 and to between three and four percent in 1970, statistical evidence on farmers' circumstances has become fuller. During the first half of the twentieth century, about one-third of farmers were tenant farmers, between one-third and two-fifths of all farms were mortgaged, and farm labor attained the less than munificent average monthly wage of about $45. Before World War II the net income of farms in the twentieth century averaged about $800 per year.

Industrial workers, who on the eve of the Civil War made up about thirty percent of the nation's labor force, increased to almost forty percent by 1900, when their numbers finally surpassed those of farmers. As the economy became increasingly sophisticated in the twentieth century, trade and service industries became more prevalent but the proportion of industrial workers held firm. (The new workers, many of them white collar, in effect replaced the disappearing agricultural labor force.) Industrial labor's wages for most of American history have not been impressive. At mid-nineteenth century, skilled workers were earning no more than nine to ten dollars per week, unskilled workers slightly more than half that rate. A generation later, wages had risen by about thirty-five percent. A nice indication of how modestly industrial labor fared in the late nineteenth century is the fact that what biographers call the small or modest wages of President Eisenhower's father when he worked in his brother-in-law's creamery were nevertheless between four and five times as much as the average worker earned.

Since local tax assessors and federal census takers used to report the value of the real estate and the personal property individuals owned, historians have been able to gather a great deal of information on the distribution of wealth in the nation during the first century after independence. Scholars have described the inequality disclosed by the evidence as "shocking" or "appalling."

Most families during this century were not down and out and yet, according to census enumerators and tax assessors, they owned nothing that had any market value whatever. In contrast, the wealthiest families lived lives that matched the lavish lifestyles of European capitalists and aristocrats. For most of the period, the richest one percent of American families owned close to half the nation's wealth and the richest ten percent owned about nine-tenths of the wealth. That people evidently lied to officials about the true value of their possessions suggests that men who claimed they were worth "nothing" probably were worth something. Yet inequality may have been even more glaring than the figures indicate, since wealthy property owners had by far the most to conceal and lie about. In the absence of direct evidence on the value of people's possessions in the twentieth century, scholars have had to make estimates based on other, less comprehensive evidence. Wealth continues to be unequally distributed—drastically so—but if the rate of inequality among individuals seems to have diminished during the past seventy-five years, it appears to signify not so much a truly equalizing trend as it does the cleverness of the wealthy in getting around modern inheritance taxes.

Recent evidence on income complements earlier evidence on property ownership in establishing the persistence of a dramatic inequality of material circumstances in American history. Immediately after the end of World War II, one-half of the nation's families earned less than $3,000 per year, four-fifths made less than $5,000, and fewer than three percent earned $10,000 or more a year. As for single individuals, about ninety percent at the war's end earned less than $3,000 and only one percent made $10,000 per year or more. By 1970 two-thirds of these individuals still made less than $5,000 per annum and fewer than one-tenth earned $10,000 or more. Truly high incomes were, with the exception of the earnings of stars in the entertainment and amusement industries, pretty much confined to business, finance, medicine, and the law.

Evidence for the twentieth century reveals how very few people are ever engaged in business management or the lucrative professions. That no more than one-third of one percent—not of the total population but of the more restrictive group, the total labor force—have been lawyers, doctors, or corporate officials suggests that, insofar as occupation is a clue to an individual's class position, scholarly estimates that place ten to twelve percent of the population in the upper three classes if anything underestimate the actual imbalance in the American class structure and exaggerate the proportions belonging to these upper clusters.

The accessibility of college, university, and professional school attendance in American history also appears to have been greatly exaggerated in popular thinking. For if such attendance by young people were truly a characteristic of upper middle, lower upper, and upper upper class families, then membership in these classes would be even more exclusive than we think it is. Before the Civil War, less than one percent of the eligible young population (aged 18 to 24) attended college. In 1900 the figure was still under three percent, while by 1940 it was not yet ten percent. As for attendance at such prestigious schools as Yale, Dartmouth, Princeton, Harvard, Columbia, William and Mary, Virginia, Brown, Amherst, and the University of Pennsylvania, the figures when combined constitute a minuscule fraction of one percent for any year before the twentieth century. These were truly exclusive institutions.

Although many scholars cite religious affiliation, too, as an indicator of class, I hesitate to do so in view of the disparate social groups that belong to each church or denomination. No poor men are bankers or send their children to exclusive private schools (in the absence of scholarships) but some poor men and their families do belong to so-called "high prestige" denominations—there are rich Catholics and poor, wealthy Jews and poor. Nevertheless, such Protestant churches as the Episcopalian and the Presbyterian provide a clue to upper-class standing, enrolling as they typically do less than two percent of the population and composed as they have primarily been of persons involved in the lucrative and prestigious occupations.

The point of this discussion of a variety of disparate indicators of a family's or an individual's class position is to suggest that the sociological estimates of the percentages of American population belonging in each of the six classes at mid-twentieth century do not appear to exaggerate the imbalance that has actually prevailed in the class structure over the course of American history.

These estimates lead us to the climactic question. How does the distribution of the general population in the American class structure compare with the distribution of the presidents' families in that structure? In order to answer that question it is necessary to assign each presidential family its appropriate niche in the social order. On the basis of the evidence set forth in the previous chapter, readers can make their own rankings and compare them with mine.

I rank the presidential families as follows, working from the top down: in the upper upper class, I place the families of Washington, Jefferson, Madison, John Quincy Adams, William Henry Harrison, Tyler, Taylor, Benjamin Harrison, Theodore Roosevelt, Taft, and Franklin D. Roosevelt; in a category straddling the upper upper and lower upper classes, the families of Polk and Kennedy; in the lower upper class, the families of John Adams, Monroe, and Wilson; on a plateau between the lower upper and the upper middle classes, the families of Pierce, Hayes, Cleveland, Harding, Coolidge, and Truman; in the upper middle class, the families of Jackson, Van Buren, Buchanan, Grant, Arthur, McKinley, Hoover, Lyndon Johnson, Ford, and Carter; in the "true" middle or between the upper and lower middle classes, the families of Lincoln, Eisenhower, and Reagan; in the lower middle class, the families of Fillmore, Garfield, and Nixon; and alone in a lower class—but in the upper lower—the family of Andrew Johnson.

These do not purport to be precise rankings; I must admit that I arranged them slightly differently one year ago. Knowledgeable persons are sure to disagree in this or that particular. But I believe my rankings are close to the mark. If Jefferson's father was not quite at the very top in Albemarle County, his mother's family was one of the greatest in all of Virginia. The family into which John Quincy Adams was born had been exalted both by his father's political achievements and the "strain of aristocracy" in his mother's line. Standing between the Kennedys and membership in the very highest class were subtle questions about the Irish Catholicism and the nouveau character of the paternal line, for all the family's great wealth, influence, and increasing access to the higher echelons of Massachusetts society. The prestige and attainments of the Wilsons more than compensated for the absence of lavish wealth. If several of the other rankings raise questions and/or eyebrows, it is only because earlier valuations of these presidential families underestimated their wealth, prestige, and influence, on the one hand, while exaggerating the condition and standing of the general population, on the other.

If one thinks of upper-middle-class families as those hovering near the bottom of the upper tenth, then my placement of the Grants, Arthurs, Hoovers, Fords, and Carters may well treat them too modestly, in view of the higher standing in their communities that their unusual wealth, political influence, voluntary association activities, or their prestige earned for them. Neither in wealth nor in the level of his community involvements was Abraham Lincoln's father akin to the lower half of the population among which he lived. And in view of Jacob Johnson's evident popularity with influential men in his community, his place in the town constabulary, and the achievements of some members of his wife's family, it is possible that I have ranked the family of the seventeenth president too modestly.

One thing is clear. The popular assumption that most of the presidents were of humble birth is wrong. No matter what changes might be made in the class ranking of one or another presidential family, the general pattern remains: the families of the presidents were strikingly dissimilar in their social and economic circumstances to most American families. In contrast to the three percent of the general population who were in the upper classes, fifty percent of the presidents' families belonged at the top. Where slightly more than one-tenth of the families of the people were in the three highest classes, almost nine-tenths of the families of our highest leaders were to be found there. And while about half the general population were in the lower classes, only one presidential family ranked so low and even they were not on the very lowest rung. The families of our highest leaders have stood far above the families of the people they led.

Several questions arise. What accounts for the great differences between the families of the presidents and the people? What is the significance of these disparities? And why have we so long clung to false beliefs about the allegedly humble origins and the social representativeness of the presidents? No brief discussion can do full justice to questions as complex as these. And yet no serious report comparing the social and economic situations of the leaders and the led can refrain from some comment, no matter how glancing, on the implications of the evidence.

The clearest part of any answer to the question, Why have the presidents' youthful circumstances been so unlike those of the American people?, is that the dissimilarity does not seem to be due to mere chance. The unrelenting nonrepresentation in the highest office of the numerically preponderant elements in the American population cannot be attributed to a statistically inexplicable roll of the political dice. Upper- or close to upper-crust family standing has obviously been advantageous to candidates for the nation's most exalted post. Paradoxically, the major parties that since George Washington's time have nominated every successful candidate for the presidency do not appear to have sought men of privileged beginnings or even to have been much interested in what these beginnings may have been. Yet these parties and the men who have run them have well understood that political gold in plebeian origins of the candidates they place before the electorate. That they have nevertheless bypassed men of such origins indicates that other things than catering to the public's presumed attraction to men of humble origins were on the minds of party managers. Above all they appear to have sought likely winners but likely winners possessed of what they regard as "sound" social values and beliefs. For if a potential candidate's ideas were considered dangerous or unacceptable, he would not do, no matter how intelligent and attractive he might be or might by artful propaganda be made to seem to be.

In choosing candidates for the presidency—and for that matter for other elective office, at all levels of government—the parties appear to have acted on the premise that men who have thrived under the American society's prevailing arrangements are most likely to have the appropriately "sound" beliefs. That is, the parties almost invariably select men who, as adults, are in the higher echelons inhabited by perhaps ten percent of the population. The interest of the nominators is in their candidates' adult, not their youthful, circumstances. Now, were upward mobility or the rise from rags to riches as commonplace as popular belief has long insisted it was, a fair sprinkling of poor boys could be expected to have attained whatever degree of success was typically necessary for presidential nominees. But such upward movement turns out rarely to have been the case. Our presidents have had unusually comfortable early circumstances because such circumstances were usually necessary to achieve the kind of success, whether in politics or elsewhere, that in the eyes of America's major parties made men the stuff of candidates for the highest office.

That not one Jew, black, or "ethnic" and only one Catholic has held the office, in a nation composed largely of these groups, is explained in part by prejudice, in part by the rules of the presidential electoral process, and in part by a law of statistics. Numerous studies testify to the persistence of racial, religious, and national or ethnic bigotry in the United States. Yet, members of maligned minorities do get elected in fair numbers to the Congress as well as to local and state legislative bodies. And where a smaller community's unusual racial, religious, and ethnic balance or its equally unusual liberal political ideology permits, members of pariah minority groups are even elected to the community's highest office. But the principle of "proportional representation" that secures unpopular minorities *some* representation in a relatively large legislative body does not apply in an election of one chief executive. And the nation as a whole is most unlike communities that are composed largely of minorities or of people who are strikingly offbeat in their beliefs. A presidential election—and, for that matter, a presidential selection by a major party—is what statisticians would call a form of "sampling with replacement." That is, each time the process recurs, every four years, a brand new ball game in effect takes place. (In a sampling *without* replacement, the selection of individuals with certain distinctive traits improves the chances of individuals with other traits in subsequent selections.) Presidential nominating bodies approach each nomination afresh, looking—as did their predecessors four years earlier—for men (not women) of sound social mind and what they consider to be the racial, ethnic, and religious credentials necessary for a winner. The Catholic nominees Al Smith and John F. Kennedy seem at this point only to have been the exceptions that prove this rule of presidential politics.

The comparatively privileged origins of the presidents throw interesting light on American politics and society. Clearly the opportunity of those born poor and in lackluster circumstances to rise to the very heights of prestige and power is far more limited than we had thought. In view of the great political advantages conferred on wealth and social eminence, it seems equally clear that democracy in the United States has a surprisingly aristocratic cast to its makeup.

Now it is true that when the entire period of our national history is closely analyzed, it becomes apparent that a significant change has occurred during the past century. Presidents born into the upper upper class have become more rare, those born into the upper middle more characteristic. The truly poor and lower middle, however, continue to be bypassed. The facts suggest that the slightly more plebeian starting points of latter-day presidents testify perhaps less strongly to the democratization of the political process than to the slightly greater chances more recently available to persons born into the lower levels of the *upper* social clusters. Despite slight changes in the patterns of the presidents' social origins, from one period in our history to another, the central fact, now as earlier, remains the almost total exclusion of men born to poor or modest stations.

The popularity nevertheless of the myth that most presidents have had humble origins tells interesting things about the American social mind. It indicates our lack of interest in facts—in this instance, facts long available—that might detract from our charming version of our national past. It reveals our disinclination to analyze critically an idea that has been so comforting to the national ego. It illuminates how foggy have been our notions about class, how much we have exaggerated the attractiveness of most people's circumstances and their opportunities to ascend to the social or political heights. It suggests that the media, which play so great a role in shaping the public's consciousness, are perfectly willing to propagate myths likely to have a stabilizing effect on our political life, no matter how slight the factual basis of these myths. That there is good reason to wonder whether the popular delusion about the presidents' modest beginnings will be dispelled, even by the broadcasting of conclusive evidence to the contrary, suggests that the actual facts play a surprisingly small part in shaping the American people's convictions concerning their nation's past.

☆☆☆☆☆ CHAPTER FOUR ☆☆☆☆☆

Prepresidential Careers

A POPULAR AMERICAN BELIEF holds that presidents are ordinary men who have taken on an extraordinary job. A sensible president supposedly "never forgets that he is just an average citizen raised temporarily to high office." Complementing—or is it, rather, contradicting?—this belief is the equally popular view that presidents are, in Harold Laski's phrase, "uncommon men of common opinions." Actually, these beliefs are not mutually exclusive. For the "uncommonness" in question refers to traits of intellect and character, while the ordinariness has to do with social standing and economic circumstances. The intelligence and the characters of the presidents are beyond the scope of this inquiry and shall be treated only glancingly. This chapter examines rather the social and economic standing attained by the presidents prior to the time when they were "raised temporarily to high office."

The whole world knows what Washington, Jackson, Teddy Roosevelt, Eisenhower, and Reagan did before they became president. Since, however, some popular notions about even the most celebrated of the presidents are inaccurate as well as incomplete, I have thought it useful to sketch in some of the vital details of all their adult careers rather than merely summarize these careers or break them down into occupational categories. Summaries have of course been published, documenting the number of presidents who attended college or became lawyers or held local or national office. A problem with such catalogues is their failure to indicate the oftentimes diverse activities of a single individual, not to mention their inability to capture the level within a given occupation or activity that was attained by a future president. No mere summary of presidential occupations will reveal the very special standing Herbert Hoover attained as engineer, William Howard Taft as lawyer, or Woodrow Wilson as teacher and scholar. To understand fully the social backgrounds of the presidents, it is necessary to know the important, unique details highlighting their prepresidential careers.

Knowing as we do that most of the presidents were born to families of unusually high standing and material well-being, it might seem that their fortunate starting points almost assured their own subsequent success. But a moment's reflection undermines this assumption. Men born to high place can themselves stumble. For that matter, whatever success they manage to achieve cannot automatically be attributed to their fortunate infancy and youth. It is conceivable that someone born to privilege might have succeeded in the absence of his inherited social and economic advantages. While the evidence does not permit us to speak with total assurance, it does help to clarify what it was that enabled the presidents to achieve their success.

I would make two additional points before proceeding to descriptions of the presidents' prepresidential careers. A number of the presidents evidently delighted in poor-mouthing themselves. Washington described himself as "cash poor" and had to borrow $500 before departing for New York City and the presidency. John Adams professed to be worried about his wife's economic future. Jefferson at one point in his remarkably successful career claimed to be impoverished. Monroe complained of money shortage. John Tyler sold a female slave in order to raise cash on the eve of his departure for the United States Senate. At a time in his youth when he was able to invest $70,000, Theodore Roosevelt bemoaned not having "butter and jam" to put on his bread. The comfortably situated Taft declaimed on the "happiness of poverty," a poverty he himself was ostensibly experiencing. Doris

Kearns has remarked on Lyndon Johnson's delight in professing youthful poverty. In view of the actual circumstances of each of these men, it seems wise not to put too much stock in these claims to calamity.

It is true that the presidents, like other men, had careers which, if not checkered, were not unbroken successes. In the vignettes that follow, I have stressed both the dominant trend in their adult careers and the destinations they reached just prior to their election to the presidency or—for the men who had suddenly to replace a stricken or fallen president—the vice-presidency.

These vignettes are not equal in length. Where the conventional wisdom about the prepresidential career of one of the better known of the presidents is essentially accurate, the account of that career is presented succinctly. Where the career was a complex one, not easily categorized, I thought it wise to present the evidence in richer detail. Understanding the place in the American social and economic order achieved, say, by Chester A. Arthur before he attained the highest office, is enhanced by knowledge of his diverse career, the more nuanced such knowledge the better.

George Washington's circumstances changed markedly for the better after his marriage to Martha Dandridge Custis. No longer a minor planter, he now moved into "another economic sphere." Yet his earlier situation was hardly plebeian. Born to wealth and advantage, he became a county surveyor at eighteen; it was hardly because of need that he engaged in this "remunerative profession." As a young man he belonged to the small group of large property owners, each of whom owned thousands of acres, and when his brother's widow died, Washington became the owner of Mount Vernon. Furnishing his home with "rare taste and elegance," and maintaining it with a large corps of servants and slaves in the years before he was given command of the Patriot army during the Revolution, Washington bred horses, joined with his fellow aristocrats in hunting foxes on the average of one day per week, and entertained lavishly about three hundred guests a year. Wealthy enough to be "something of a private banker" to his fellow aristocrats, Washington also performed the public services and held the public offices that were monopolized by the social and economic elite in colonial Virginia. Serving as vestryman in his Anglican church, member of the House of Burgesses, trustee of the town of Alexandria, and justice of the county court, Washington appears to have been in every sense a leading member of Virginia's most select circle.

On graduating from Harvard, the future second president returned to Braintree, Massachusetts, as John Adams, "Esquire." After working for a short time in Worcester as a schoolmaster, he embarked at twenty on the study of law. As a young man he studied with Jeremiah Gridley, "the most eminent lawyer" in Boston, and in a very short time gained prominence in the profession. By the time he was thirty-one, Adams was recognized as one of the leading members of the Massachusetts bar, arguing cases of high importance; he was offered the prestigious position of advocate general of the Court of Admiralty, an offer he turned down. In subsequently "bemoaning" his alleged lack of sufficient savings, despite his great success, Adams, according to one biographer, "lapsed into one of his spells of self-pity." His situation did not justify his pessimism. Like Washington, the young Adams had for a short time been a surveyor—of highways in Braintree—after being left property by his father. He subsequently served as one of six selectmen for his township. Elected in 1770 as delegate to the general court or the assembly of Massachusetts, Adams was shortly afterwards named to the Continental Congress and became one of the leading political figures in the Patriot cause during the Revolution and in the years immediately after. He served as wartime commissioner to France, minister plenipotentiary to negotiate the end of the fighting, first American ambassador to St. James after the fighting stopped, and vice-president under Washington.

The most important fact of Thomas Jefferson's young adult years, according to his most distinguished biographer, was the "assured financial position" provided by his great landholdings. When at nineteen he studied law, he did so with George Wythe, "the best classical scholar in Virginia," and when the young Jefferson took up the practice of the profession his clients were Randolphs, Pages, Carys, Harrisons, Lees, Byrds, and other members of the best families of Virginia. The young Jefferson, studying music, dancing, and classical learning and culture with private tutors and at William and Mary College, was "father" to Thomas Jefferson, the Renaissance man of his mature years. Inheriting tens of thousands of profitable acres, dozens of slaves, and a lucrative water mill on coming of age, Jefferson was already one of the richest men in Albemarle County, Virginia, even before his marriage. Like Washington before him, he became very much richer still through his wife. Jefferson's very expensive tastes, which he indulged "in spite of all his moralizing" about the simple life, intermittently saddled him with nagging debts, as did "the burdens" of the great Wayles estate which his marriage brought him. These, however, were the debts of a hugely rich man, living the sybaritic life at Monticello and abroad and in no sense prevented from doing so by these financial problems. As one of the five wealthiest young men in Albemarle County, Jefferson was at twenty-five selected as one of two delegates to the House of Burgesses. He thereafter played the active public and political life expected "at that time and place of a young man of his estate and training," serving as justice of the peace and member of the county court, and commander of militia, among other posts. After being named a deputy to the Continental Congress in 1775, he quickly became one of the new nation's most respected figures, serving as wartime governor of Virginia, peace negotiator, Franklin's successor as ambassador to France, and Washington's first secretary of state. Breaking with the Washington Administration over domestic and foreign policy, Jefferson became the leader of an opposition party. In 1796 he was elected vice-president and four years later, president.

After graduating from Princeton University, Madison, who had studied law and theology, lived off the fruits of the plantation and the labor of the more than one hundred slaves he had inherited. Choosing not to practice law, he lived in grand style on his Montpelier estate, in a "magnificent mansion dominated by [a] classic portico." By the time he had attained national prominence as a political thinker and leader, he was enjoying a substantial income from three separate estates and profiting too from occasional modest real estate speculations. In 1775, when he was twenty-three, Madison was elected to local office in Orange County, Virginia, and during the Revolution his elections and re-elections to the new state legislature were unbroken, except for the one year 1777–1778, because "he refused to give the voters free whiskey." After serving in the Continental Congress for four years commencing in 1779, Madison returned to the Virginia legislature until 1787, when he was selected as one of the state's delegates to the Constitutional Convention. After 1788 Madison served continually as congressman or state legislator—in 1796 turning down unanimous election as governor of Virginia—until in 1801 Jefferson named him secretary of state. He succeeded Jefferson as president after 1808.

The central motif of James Monroe's career was ambition for wealth, high place, and standing. At sixteen his hopes were powerfully abetted by his inheritance of all his father's not insubstantial property and by his increasingly close relationship with his uncle, the influential Judge Joseph Jones, who was the executor of Monroe's estate. As an able young soldier and diplomat during the Revolution, who was much esteemed by Washington, Monroe was high-minded but also wealthy enough to forgo all compensation for many of his early public services. In common with the aristocratic pattern in which young men prepared for the law under the tutelage of great eminences, Monroe read for the law with Jefferson. Not that Monroe was much interested either in legal theory or practice; he took law up as the career "offering the most immediate rewards" and as the stepping-stone to office, standing, and wealth. Monroe was an active and successful accumulator of western lands, patenting more than 100,000 acres in Kentucky alone in the years immediately after the Revolution. He married into the aristocracy of New York, maintained an expensive and elegant establishment, and was snob enough to be furious with a social acquaintance, who was not of the very highest standing, when this man permitted his daughter to marry one of Monroe's younger brothers. Such a marriage, Monroe believed, "made it unlikely that his brother would make a name for himself."

For all his lands, slaves, possessions, and social standing,

Monroe was intermittently beset by debts, some of them not of his own making, and was often short of ready cash. Such problems meant, not the possibility of debtors' prison, but the necessity only of selling this number of slaves or disposing of that number of acres. Like his great Virginia predecessors, Monroe entered politics as a young man, at twenty-four seeking a seat in the Virginia House of Delegates, "because membership in the legislature was essential for a young man anxious to advance his fortune and his career." That career was abetted by the support he received from great figures such as Lord Sterling, Washington, and Jefferson, as Monroe moved from state to national office, serving in ambassadorships, the Virginia governor's office, and the Madison administration both as secretary of state and for a short time, simultaneously, as secretary of war. In 1816 he succeeded Madison, as the last of the "Virginia Dynasty."

When John Quincy Adams was born in 1767, his father was of course not yet the president. The elder Adams was, however, a thriving and prosperous lawyer at the time of his son's birth and was soon to be a great political figure in the new nation. John Adams was thus able to afford his son not simply a comfortable youth but a magnificent education at the hands of private tutors and the uniquely rich cultural experience that went with staying with his father during the latter's travels and diplomatic engagements in Europe. When, after graduating from Harvard, the younger Adams's early law practice did not thrive, he could fall back on his father's generous subsidy until business picked up. John Quincy Adams's career, even as a youth, was devoted almost entirely to political service, for he early showed great flair when called on to assist his father. Drawn into the diplomatic service, first by Washington, as minister to Holland, and then by his father, as minister to Prussia, Adams returned in 1801 to Boston. He now took up an almost unbroken political career, first as state senator, then as United States senator (during which time he also held a professorship in rhetoric and oratory at Harvard), minister to Russia, peace commissioner to negotiate the end of the War of 1812, minister to England, and secretary of state under Monroe. In 1825 he was elected president by vote of the House of Representatives, after failing to win a majority of the electoral votes for the high office.

In popular mythology, Andrew Jackson was a rough backcountry Indian fighter, whose election to the presidency at sixty-one was due to his plebeian career and character as well as to his outstanding military leadership. In fact, Andrew Jackson was indeed a successful Indian fighter and the Hero of New Orleans, but there was little that was plebeian about his circumstances or values. Born to unusual advantages, even as a boy of fifteen he belonged, according to one biographer, "to all the aristocracy there was in the back country"—"the owners of slaves, the breeders of horses, the holders of local offices and titles." When as a young man not yet twenty he read for the law, he did so first with Spruce Macay, an unusually wealthy lawyer, and subsequently with Col. John Stokes, a brilliant as well as eminent attorney. As a young lawyer in Nashville, Jackson was hell on debtors, enforcing many writs of execution, functioning precisely as "the kind of lawyer the property owners of Nashville wanted." By his early twenties he was well on the way himself to becoming a substantial property owner, "embarking on many schemes for the accumulation of a fortune," of the sort not usually resorted to by a professional man. Aligning himself with the wealthiest and most influential "power brokers" in Tennessee, Jackson was "alert to any scheme that would augment his income." He dealt in slaves, made hundreds of thousands of dollars and accumulated hundreds of thousands of valuable acres in land speculation, owned racehorses and racetracks, bought cotton gins, distilleries, and plantations, was a successful merchant, and married extremely well. In the words of a biographer, "an urge to riches and social rank seemed to impel this activity." A bad experience with a defaulting merchant at one point in his business career put him in some financial straits and further hardened his attitude of unrelenting lack of sympathy for commercial debt. Jackson easily survived what was a temporary and modest setback, going on to thrive anew, own more than one hundred slaves, and live and entertain sumptuously at the Hermitage on his estate outside of Nashville. Jackson's appointments to his early military and political positions owed a great deal, if not everything, to his wealth and to the elite circle he moved in. Judge, district attorney general, militia officer, member of the House of Representatives and of the U.S. Senate from Tennessee, member of the state supreme court, major general of the army, governor of Florida, again United States senator—from which exalted legislative position friends hoped he could vault into a yet more exalted executive position in the White House—Jackson's public like his private career was marked by nearly unbroken success prior to his losing race for the presidency in 1824. Four years later, capitalizing on his charge that he had been wrongfully denied his proper place at the head of the nation by a "corrupt bargain" between Adams and Henry Clay, Jackson was swept into the White House.

In the autobiography that he began to write late in life, Martin Van Buren said: "I was not worth a shilling when I began my professional career." Actually, as a young teenager he had attended a private academy and at age 15 or 16—Van Buren could not remember which was accurate—he was "placed in a lawyer's office where [he] remained for several years." He studied not with some humdrum rural attorney but with Francis Silvester, a man of "much reputation and distinction." The eighth president is widely and accurately known as a politician par excellence, devoting most of his life to that calling, first in New York State and then in the nation's capital. But much of his early political career overlapped with his career as an attorney. After completing his course of study with the eminent William P. Van Ness at age 20, Van Buren began to practice law and continued actively in the profession for the next twenty-five years. For all his preoccupation with politics over much of this period, Van Buren quickly became an inordinately successful—because he was an inordinately able—lawyer. He early won the distinction of admittance as a counselor of the state supreme court, built an admired and lucrative practice based on his mastery of "intricate" aspects of the craft, was associated with—or opposed by—lawyers of the caliber and distinction of Peter Van Schaack, Thomas Addis Emmet, David B. Ogden, and Aaron Burr, the crème de la crème of the New York bar, as well as the mighty Daniel Webster of New Hampshire and

Massachusetts. According to one of his early biographers, Van Buren "left the bar with a competence fairly earned, which his prudence and skill made grow into an ample fortune." He put part of his growing fortune into New York real estate that rapidly appreciated in value and he won a well-earned and unshakeable reputation as a dandy by his fastidious and expensive tastes in food, clothing, home furnishings, and what we nowadays call lifestyle. His political offices through middle age, while increasingly exalted, do not begin to suggest his great political power. Commencing at age 25 as a surrogate of Columbia County, five years later he was named New York state senator; two years after that, attorney general; six years later, U.S. senator; and then, at age 45, governor of New York. For most of this time Van Buren was the unrivaled head of the "Regency," the small political machine that controlled what was first the Republican and subsequently the Democratic party of the nation's wealthiest and most populous state. With the election of Andrew Jackson to the presidency, Van Buren, who had played a crucial part in organizing the national coalition responsible for Jackson's victory, was named secretary of state. Four years later he was named Jackson's running mate in his successful contest for a second term and in 1836 was chosen by Jackson, the party, and the nation to occupy the White House.

Born to one of the wealthiest and most eminent families in Virginia, William Henry Harrison, "contrary to the family custom," went to Hampton-Sidney College rather than William and Mary. Neither the length of his stay nor his reasons for attending are clear; certainly he was no scholar. When his father died, it was decided that young Harrison should take up medicine and study in Philadelphia under the guardianship of the famous Robert Morris. He was sent at seventeen to the Quaker city to study under Dr. William Shippen, president of the College of Physicians in the University of Pennsylvania, and the great Benjamin Rush. Disliking medicine, young Harrison decided to take up a military career instead and through the support he received from Virginia Governor Richard Henry Lee was at eighteen commissioned ensign in the U.S. infantry. Later John Quincy Adams would say of the mature Harrison that he had a "faculty of making friends" whom he was "incessantly importuning for their influence in his favor." Although Adams thought him a man "not without talents," he also thought him vain, indiscreet, and possessed of a lively "but shallow mind." However that may be, it does seem that before his election to the presidency in 1840 at age 67, Harrison's career had been essentially a disappointment, particularly in view of his initial advantages.

Judged by ordinary standards, however, it was a very successful career. Named governor of the Indiana territory when he was twenty-seven, Harrison employed his large salary to engage in various "schemes to augment his income," dabbling in land speculation, mills, a shipyard, and an exporting company, among other interests. His marriage at twenty-two to Anna Symmes, daughter of Judge John Cleve Symmes, one of the largest land speculators in the Northwest territory, abetted his search for the good life. Owners of an expensive and impressive brick house in Vincennes, the Harrisons dispensed lavish hospitality, yet Harrison's later financial and business career was beset by significant setbacks that compelled him to sell thousands of acres of land and other properties in order to meet debt payments. After a military career that saw him rise from ensign through the ranks of lieutenant, captain, major general first of the Kentucky militia and then of the 8th military district, and finally, brigadier general, Harrison resigned from the army in 1814 at age 41. There is something pathetic in the spectacle of the "Hero of the Battle of the Thames" in the War of 1812 scrounging for relatively petty public positions in the years after the war. And yet by ordinary standards, Harrison's political career prior to his rise to the presidency was hardly a failure, including as it did the territorial governorship, membership in the U.S. House of Representatives and the senate both of Ohio and the nation, as well as a brief—and ineffectual—stint as minister to Colombia. But of course Harrison had extraordinary advantages. Adams was not the only contemporary to ridicule Harrison's "positively rabid" thirst for "lucrative office," his many rejections, even for minor posts, and his scrambling in his sixty-first year for the situation as clerk of the court of common pleas of Hamilton County in his quest to lighten his financial difficulties. There is something pathetic too in Harrison's evident reliance—at the time he was elected to the highest office—on a fund provided by Abbott Lawrence of Massachusetts and other capitalists to help him meet his private expenses. A sympathetic biographer thinks it probable that these secret handouts placed Harrison under "obligations to these men."

In the fashion of the time, John Tyler entered college at thirteen. The college was of course William and Mary. Also in the fashion of the time—at least for the nation's blue bloods—when he read for the law, after graduation, he did so under men of great distinction, first with his father and then, when the elder Tyler became Governor of Virginia, with the even more eminent Edmund Randolph, attorney general and secretary of war in the Washington administrations. Not accidentally, for a young lawyer trained by men of such repute, Tyler quickly built up a lucrative practice. Before he was twenty-six Tyler was earning more than three times as much as the ambitious and successful Daniel Webster. Again, in the best upper-crust tradition, Tyler combined private career with public service. At twenty-one he was elected to the Virginia House of Delegates—the lower house of the state legislature—and after serving five successive terms, resigned in 1815 to become a member of the council of state, the eight-member body that functioned as cabinet or advisors to the governor of Virginia. After serving five years in the House of Representatives, he returned to his private practice for two years before resuming his place in the House of Delegates. In 1826, at thirty-five, Tyler was named governor and, during his second term, U.S. senator. He served in the senate for nine years before resigning in 1836, was elected again to the House of Delegates in 1838, and the following year, after being defeated for the state's Whig Party senate nomination, was named by the national party as William Henry Harrison's running mate.

If Tyler was "often forced into uncomfortable financial straits," it was primarily because his large family "had to be maintained according to the high standard set by the landed aristocracy of Virginia." The mother of this family was Tyler's first wife, Letitia Christian, daughter of a man of "considerable property" and influential connections in the Peninsula. Robert Christian's death soon after his daughter's marriage to Tyler meant that the young couple would inherit a substantial legacy. After his wife's death, Tyler married a young woman—the beauteous Julia Gardiner—whose family had unsurpassed standing in New York City but by that time he was already in the White House. A biographer observes that Tyler had to expend no effort "in social climbing, for in his case social position was not something to be achieved but to be taken as a matter of course." Yet it was conceivable that he could have stumbled. As his many critics would exclaim, he did indeed stumble, politically. But not socially.

After graduating from the University of North Carolina at Chapel Hill, James Knox Polk quickly achieved outstanding success, both as lawyer and as politician. Before he was thirty, he had, according to his most thorough biographer, become "one of the most successful young lawyers in Tennesee," earning in a good year half as much again as did that prominent young lawyer, John Tyler of Virginia. An "intimate of the state's most prominent men," Polk was named a colonel of the militia, he was a leader of the state legislature, and at twenty-nine he was elected to Congress. Polk was in the national House of Representatives from 1825 to 1839, serving as speaker of the house for the last four of these years. Governor of Tennessee between 1839 and 1841, Polk was defeated in his bid for reelection. Although he became known as the first "dark horse" candidate when nominated by the Democrats for the presidency in 1844, the fact is that he won the nomination only because of his comparative prominence as a national as well as state political figure. Polk's high ambition and his yearning for life's good things were both enhanced by his marriage to Sarah Childress, a plain young woman but one who was considered "something of a catch." For her father, Major Joel Childress, was a wealthy man of diverse business and landed interests, who entertained Tennessee's most prominent citizens on his plantation just outside the state capitol. James and Sarah Polk inherited slaves and large properties in Tennessee and Alabama on Childress's death.

Zachary Taylor has been described by his leading biographer

as a "planter to the manner born." When at twenty-six he married Margaret Mackall Smith, of a "prominent Maryland family," Taylor's present from his father was an attractive landed property. Taylor subsequently bought land in Mississippi as well as Kentucky, where he lived as an adult, not only accumulating thousands of acres but making profits of tens of thousands of dollars from the lands he sold. At the end of the Mexican War, during which his military feats made him a national hero, Taylor was one of that elite group of no more than eighteen hundred planters—or a fraction of one percent of the adult white male population in the South—who owned more than one hundred slaves each. Profiting from warehouses, urban lots, and bank stock, as well as from land and slaves, Taylor was a very rich man by the time of his elevation to the presidency. Informed contemporaries estimated the value of his property to be in the neighborhood of $200,000, a sum that, given the adjusted value of the dollar, made Taylor the equivalent of a modern millionaire many times over. A volunteer in the Kentucky militia before the age of twenty, almost all of Taylor's adult life was spent in the army after he was in 1808 made a lieutenant. During that forty-year period, he was promoted to captain, rose to major during the War of 1812, and resigned from the army after being reduced to captain at the end of the war; he was reappointed the following year at the higher rank, became a colonel during the Black Hawk War of the early 1830s, a brevet brigadier general during the second Seminole War, and, during the Mexican War, a major general after his victories at Palo Alto and Monterey. In accord with the American tradition that offers the highest political office to a hero of the last war, regardless of his inexperience in statecraft, Taylor was nominated by the Whigs and won the presidency in 1848.

Millard Fillmore, who moved into the White House on Taylor's death in 1850, was the first president who suffered something close to poverty during his youth. According to Fillmore himself, his early life on his family's farm was so hard that from ten or eleven on, he was permitted to attend school only two or three months a year, in the winter, because his labor could not be spared during the warm weather months. Since his father's grim experience trying to farm poor soil had led him to the decision that his sons "should follow some other occupation" than farming and since "his means did not justify . . . aspiring to any profession," young Fillmore was at fourteen sent off to be an apprentice to a man some distance from his home who was in the "business of carding and cloth-dressing" and the following year to a tradesman nearer to his father's residence. He served more than three years of this apprenticeship, interspersing it with work in a sawmill and a brief and evidently unrewarding stint as a teacher in a "rough and uncultivated" country school. When he was not yet nineteen, Fillmore began to read law with the successful attorney Judge Walter Wood. After quarreling with Wood, Fillmore continued his studies for several years before being admitted to the bar at twenty-three. Very much the upwardly mobile man, Fillmore achieved quick success in his chosen profession, first in the small town of East Aurora, where during the next seven years he became the leading citizen of the community and "helped set the town's social and political tone." This pattern was repeated when Fillmore moved to Buffalo, the firm he formed with two other men soon becoming the leading law firm in that thriving city. It dissolved only in 1847, one year before Fillmore was named vice-presidential candidate on the Whig party's national ticket.

Fillmore would later say that the injustices he suffered as an apprentice made him "feel for the weak and unprotected, and hate the insolent tyrant in every station of life." Now it is true that when he was twenty-eight and a member of the New York State legislature, Fillmore was the leader of the political movement to abolish imprisonment for debt. Yet his adult lifestyle—marked as it was by formal dinners, dances, recitals, hobnobbing with celebrities, his leadership of socially prestigious voluntary associations—and a political career devoted largely to pursuit of the main chance suggest that his early difficulties filled him above all with the desire to live a comfortable material life that would be as far removed as possible from his youthful deprivation. The adult Fillmore was among the richest one percent of New York wealthholders—he was indeed able to turn his back on the hard life. Appointed in 1828 to the lucrative post of commissioner of deeds for East Aurora, he was in a position to collect substantial fees on the numerous deeds that had to be recorded in a community where "speculators and settlers sold and resold their holdings in heated haste." Fillmore was that same year elected to the New York State assembly. Four years later at thirty-two he was elected to Congress, where he served during the next ten years. After failing to win the Whig vice-presidential nomination in 1844, despite working strenuously behind the scenes, he realized his ambition four years later, after serving briefly as New York State comptroller. When Taylor died at midterm, Fillmore succeeded to the high office.

Franklin Pierce was brought up amidst increasingly comfortable circumstances, for his father's prosperity during the future president's youth enabled the elder Pierce to entertain lavishly in the newly furnished and decorated Pierce mansion in Hillsborough, New Hampshire. After attending a number of private academies, Pierce went to Bowdoin College, rejecting Dartmouth because his father was averse to sending his son to that reputed Federalist stronghold. After spending three years reading for the law, Pierce commenced his law practice in his hometown in 1827, the same year that his father was named governor of New Hampshire. Pierce was then twenty-two. Pierce's marriage to Jane Means Appleton strengthened his ties to the privileged, for she was the daughter of the former president of Bowdoin. Related as they were to the Masons of Portsmouth and the Lawrences of Boston, the Appletons were said to be "cultured aristocrats," occupying a more rarefied social plateau than the Pierces. (In view of the success achieved by Pierce's father, I think somewhat exaggerated the view expressed by a Pierce biographer that the young couple were "ill-mated" because they ostensibly "represented two different strata of New England society.") After practicing law for only two years, Pierce set his sights on a political career. He won election first to the state legislature, where he soon became speaker, and then served both in the House and in the U.S. Senate. Alas, of his five-year service in the latter body, a biographer reports that Pierce "left as his sole legislative monument several hundred pension cases." On resigning from the Senate,

Pierce resumed his law practice in Concord, the capital of New Hampshire. His substantial earnings as a corporation lawyer appear to have owed at least as much to his family connections and his political influence as to his skill with a jury. For, as a biographer concedes, Pierce was not a great lawyer. After he was named a brigadier general during the Mexican War, in which he saw no action during his one year of service, his fortunes soared. The returned war hero's law practice thrived: "his income grew and his fame grew faster." In 1848 Pierce turned down the Democratic nomination for governor of New Hampshire. After he spoke out in favor of the Compromise of 1850, the national party nominated him for the presidency in 1852.

On graduating from Dickinson College in 1809 at eighteen, James Buchanan began to prepare for a career in the law under the tutelage of James Hopkins, "a leader of the Lancaster [Pennsylvania] bar and an attorney of state-wide reputation." He was admitted to the bar three years later and quickly began to build a lucrative practice. At twenty-three he was elected to the state assembly and six years later, in 1820, to Congress. By that time he was earning more than $8,000 a year, a considerable sum then. And in the mid-1820s Buchanan was buying property around Lancaster at sheriffs' sales, property that dramatically increased in value from one year to the next. One biographer estimates that Buchanan's estate was worth $300,000 even before he was thirty. At thirty-seven, he built "Wheatland," a rather massive "bachelor home" in Lancaster. This mansion had an "imposing brick facade," that according to an architectural historian, betokened "prosperity, success, and respectability." Buchanan took money very seriously: "practically every penny that he gave or received throughout his life he methodically recorded in his account books." According to his most authoritative biographer, Buchanan once rejected a friend's check of more than $15,000 because there was an error of ten cents in it. After supporting Andrew Jackson in 1828, Buchanan, a onetime Federalist, was rewarded by being named minister to Russia in 1831. He was elected to the U.S. Senate in 1834, serving for eleven years before being named secretary of state in the Polk administration. Defeated in his bids for the Democratic presidential nomination in 1844, 1848, and 1852, Buchanan finally succeeded in 1856, after serving three years in the most prestigious of all diplomatic posts, minister to Great Britain.

Abraham Lincoln's father and his ancestors were not quite so humble as Lincoln himself made them out to be. Yet there can be no questioning the accuracy of a biographer's conclusion that Lincoln was truly a self-made man. Before winning the Republican party nomination in 1860, Lincoln had become a prominent lawyer, attained relatively substantial wealth and high social standing, and become one of the leading political figures, first in Illinois and then in the entire west. In his youth Lincoln had worked as a rail-splitter and done a variety of chores on his father's farm, occasionally hiring himself out to do odd jobs for others. On reaching maturity and "independence," he went to work as a clerk in a store in New Salem, Illinois, for $15.00 per month and sleeping accommodations in a room behind the store. Serving as a general partner three years later in another store that sold, among other things, large quantities of liquor, Lincoln quickly ran up a sizeable debt. Not yet twenty-five, Lincoln became postmaster of New Salem but at a salary so low—slightly more than one dollar per week—that he had to take on odd jobs in order to supplement his income. Notwithstanding the modest nature of his work to that point in his life, he was elected to the state legislature in 1834. Perhaps a more important turning point in his career was his decision that year to become a lawyer. He earned his license and began to practice in two years' time. In what a biographer calls "a stroke of rare good fortune," Lincoln was immediately taken in as a partner by J. T. Stuart, who, with a previous partner, had made his firm the most successful and profitable in Springfield, assuring the young new member an abundance of clients. "Good fortune" it may have been but Lincoln's own behavior had something to do with it, since as state legislator he had been instrumental in making Springfield the capital of Illinois. Four years later Lincoln left the firm to become a junior partner to Joseph T. Logan, a move that advanced his standing in the profession. Fees were not lavish, averaging about five dollars a case. But Lincoln was a hard worker who, when he married Mary Todd in 1842, was earning more annually than did the governor of the state and almost twice as much as circuit judges.

The Todds, as bona fide Kentucky aristocracy, had much higher status than Lincoln. Mary Todd was a great-granddaughter of a Revolutionary War general, granddaughter to a Kentucky hero, and a neighbor to Henry Clay, Lincoln's idol. Her father was a businessman and political figure of "broad interests and high social standing." The bridegroom was no nonentity, however, but an able and increasingly successful lawyer and public figure in his own right. Two years after his marriage, Lincoln formed what was to be a lifetime partnership with a young lawyer, William Herndon, and within a short time the new firm was doing very well indeed. Lincoln and Herndon were employed by the Illinois Central as lobbyists, among other services, and by four other railroad corporations. Instead of five dollars per case, Lincoln's fee from Illinois Central in one memorable case was $15,000. Attorney for banks, insurance companies, gas companies, large mercantile firms, and manufacturers, regularly representing his clients before the state supreme court and in the federal courts, Lincoln in the 1850s was one of the wealthiest and most admired lawyers in a state "that boasted an array of outstanding legal talent." Like ambitious and successful lawyers after his time, he simultaneously pursued a political career. After his election to the legislature in 1834 he served four successive terms and was Whig party floor leader for most of the period. In 1846 he was elected to Congress, where he served one term before returning to his law practice in 1849. In 1858 he made his unsuccessful but memorable race for the U.S. Senate and in the summer of 1860 won the Republican party nomination for the presidency at the turbulent Chicago convention.

Lincoln's successor was indeed a self-made man. Brought up by a hardworking but impecunious mother, after his father drowned when Andrew Johnson was three, the future president was apprenticed at fourteen, bound as indentured servant to J. J. Selby, the town tailor of Raleigh, North Carolina. Although his tenure was supposed to last until he reached maturity, Johnson soon ran away and, when not yet sixteen, opened his own tailor shop in the small town of Carthage. Within two years he moved several times before arriving with his family in Greeneville, Tennessee. There, at eighteen, he married Eliza McCardle, a young orphan, daughter to a shoemaker. The young man opened up a tailoring business in the front room of a small two-room building; the back room was combination kitchen, dining room, parlor, and bedroom. The "A. Johnson Tailor Shop" began quickly to thrive—if modestly. At twenty-two he was able to buy for $1,000 a local property on which he built a home and shortly afterward a new building to house his tailor shop.

Johnson's career in local politics also fared well. Elected at twenty-one to the Greeneville Board of Aldermen, he was re-elected and then elected mayor for three successive terms. At twenty-six he moved on to the state legislature, five years later to the state senate, and in 1843 at age 34 to the House of Representatives in Washington, D.C. By this time Johnson was the absentee owner of a thriving shop managed by another man and employing a half dozen journeymen tailors. After nine years in Congress, Johnson was in 1852 elected governor of Tennessee, holding the office for two terms. He now lived in a fine brick house, "a new and spacious residence . . . with generous fireplaces, high pitched ceilings and a pleasing view from every window," and owned a hotel, other properties, and eight slaves. He moved in a social world graced by the state's elite families. In 1857 Johnson was selected for the U.S. Senate. After the Civil War broke out, Lincoln named him "military governor and brigadier general to restore Tennessee to the Union." And in 1864 Johnson replaced Hannibal Hamlin of Maine as Lincoln's running mate in the presidential contest that year.

Ulysses S. Grant's career before the Civil War was unspectacular, if not dismal, and seemed if anything to go steadily downhill. Disappointments, heartache, lack of money—if not downright poverty—seemed increasingly to be the rule. And yet a close reading of that prewar career indicates that it was featured not only by opportunities but by achievements that, if modest, were nevertheless undreamed of by the great mass of Americans laboring in fields, shops, and mills. Born to a relatively successful businessman, whose diverse enterprises expanded during Grant's youth, the future hero was educated at private schools and at seventeen sent to the U.S. Military Academy at West Point. A self-taught and slightly educated man himself, Jesse Grant was evidently determined to give his son educational advantages that he himself had lacked. West Point seemed ideal from the elder Grant's view, for in addition to its prestige, it was free and it seemingly offered an assured career to young Grant. (It also provided the future hero with a new name. Born Hiram Ulysses Grant, the youth raised no objection when the roster of newcomers listed him as U. S. Grant.) Grant was later to say he had had no wish to go to West Point and he disliked military service. Like it or not, he was good at it and he spent the next fifteen years of his life at it, first training to become an officer and then serving as one in war and peace. Grant fought in the Mexican War, during which he was promoted from second lieutenant to brevet captain. When he married at the war's end, it was to a young Southern woman of breeding and standing. Julia Dent's father, Colonel Frederick Dent, is described by a Grant biographer as "one of the Maryland aristocracy by birth, as was Mrs. Dent." Formerly a successful merchant and at the time of his daughter's marriage an equally successful planter, Grant's father-in-law owned eighteen slaves and moved in a social circle that included "the best families in St. Louis." Not that the eminence of his wife's family seemed to do much directly for Grant's career. In the years after the Mexican War, as he was transferred from Detroit to Governor's Island in New York and then, in 1852, to San Francisco, Grant found himself too short of money in his last assignment to have his wife and children join him. Two years later, at age 31, Grant resigned from the army. The Grants lived for two years in the house of Col. Dent, as the former officer took up farming and the sale of cordwood. He was hardly prospering. And yet in 1856, when he built his own house, it did have servants' quarters. For a short time Grant owned one slave. In 1858 Grant gave up farming, to do real estate collecting for one of his wife's relatives. In the years before the outbreak of the Civil War, he held nondescript jobs, including a temporary post as collector of customs in St. Louis county and a short stint as clerk in his father's Galena store for less than $1,000 per year.

Grant had no zest for more war but when it did break out, he enlisted, feeling that he owed it to the government which had trained and educated him. Entering the army in 1861, he was named colonel of the Springfield, Illinois volunteers. Grant lacked the money to buy the uniform and the horse that his rank demanded. His request for a loan of a few hundred dollars was turned down both by his father and his father-in-law. Until a Galena businessman several weeks later advanced the necessary sum, Grant was unable personally to conduct his regimental dress parades. But once he saw action, his career soared, as he moved upward, across the different levels of the general's rank. His Civil War exploits earned him wealth as well as glory. After the war, citizens of Galena raised $16,000 to build a lavishly furnished house for the Grants, Philadelphians contributed an even more expensive house, New Yorkers donated $100,000 in cash, Bostonians a library, and other admirers gave the hero fourteen horses, among other gifts. And after Johnson's impeachment, the presidency beckoned.

Rutherford B. Hayes's youth was possibly deprived, but only in the emotional sense, for he was born into a fatherless family. But he was born in the best house in Delaware, Ohio, and looked after in boyhood as in later life by his mother's younger brother Sardis Birchard, one of the richest and most influential men in the state. Birchard regularly provided substantial infusions of needed funds to Hayes the governor of Ohio as well as to Hayes the youngster, the student, the aspiring lawyer. Hayes's uncle's positive influence transcended money, for as one biographer observes, Hayes "would never be able to travel very far in Ohio without meeting someone who knew his uncle and was eager to do some favor for him because of a debt, pecuniary or social, owed to Sardis." In the phrase of another biographer, "no father could have been more faithful to his charge," Birchard shaping the youngster's career, providing most of the money for his education, and standing behind and assisting him financially as well as in other ways throughout Hayes's early career. After attending a private seminary and an expensive private academy, Hayes went to Kenyon College, graduating in 1842 at nineteen. He studied at Harvard Law School for two years, then practiced at first in his uncle's village, Lower Sandusky. Continuing to depend very heavily on his uncle's financial support, at the beginning of 1850 Hayes hung out his shingle in Cincinnati. His career then took off. He made a killing, buying real estate and valuable Virginia coal and iron lands "at a ridiculous price—about 20 cents an acre," and his law practice flourished. In 1852 Hayes married Lucy Ware Webb of a family of Virginia and Kentucky slaveowners and within two years moved into a then-expensive $5500 house. Most of the money was supplied by uncle Sardis but the house was Hayes's own. Hayes now began to mix law and investment with politics. In 1858 he was elected city solicitor of Cincinnati, after being turned down earlier as a congressional candidate by the Republican party and himself turning down a Hamilton County judgeship because of its low pay. As a lawyer and as city solicitor he was earning more than $7,000 per year. When Hayes was not reelected, he returned to private practice.

Like other men in the "era of the bloody shirt," Hayes turned his participation in the Civil War to great political advantage. Joining up in 1861 as the captain of a drilling company, Hayes rose to major of an Ohio infantry regiment, practiced law as adjutant general, and then saw action as lieutenant-colonel, colonel, and major general. After suffering a severe arm wound in combat, Hayes was elected to Congress in 1864, reelected two years later, and then elected for two terms to the Ohio governorship. Turning down certain election to the U.S. Senate in 1872, thus maintaining himself in the good graces of the powerful Ohio pols who approved of the action, he was again made governor in 1875 and the next year nominated for and elected to the presidency.

James A. Garfield, whose father died when he was only two, grew up on a farm where he did the normal chores associated with rural life and ate perhaps more and better food than did most farm boys. Typically, too, he did diverse jobs for neighbors, earning extra money for chopping wood, planting crops, working in hayfields, mowing and cradling wheat. His family may not have been rich but they did own their farm. Eliza Garfield sent him first to a private academy and then to the Western Reserve Eclectic Institute. When he went to Williams College, he studied with the renowned Mark Hopkins, the president of Williams. When he needed money to pay his final fees, Hopkins lent it to him. Garfield was older than most of the young men at college, because he had held a number of jobs before entering, among them teaching, preaching, and house building. On graduating from Williams in 1856 at age 24, he returned to teach at Western Reserve, where the following year he became the chief officer. He remained there for five years, during which time he studied enough law to be admitted to the bar in Ohio. He also served a term in the state senate. In 1858 he married Lucretia Randolph, daughter of a prominent and influential man whose family commanded higher status than the Garfields'.

Garfield had a brief but highly successful military career. Volunteering as a lieutenant-colonel of the Ohio volunteer infantry, he rose within two years to the rank of major general, attaining prominence both for success in battle as a brigade commander and for his performance as chief of staff to General William Rosecrans's army. Elected to Congress in 1862 while still a general, he took up his seat on resigning from the army in 1863, and held it until 1880. While in Congress, he accepted many private cases which, together with his successful oil land purchases and his government salary, made him a very affluent man. He was a prominent man, too, for he served as House minority leader during the last three years of his term. In 1880, the Ohio legislature elected him to the U.S. Senate. But Garfield was not to serve in the upper house, since later that year he was elected president as the "dark horse" candidate of the Republican party.

The child of a successful minister, Chester A. Arthur received an unusually good education. As a boy not yet ten, he attended a private academy in Union Village and when his family moved to Schenectady, he spent a year at the lyceum, prior to entering Union College. To help defray his college expenses, he taught school part-time during his winter vacations. After graduating from Union when he was not yet eighteen, he almost immediately got a job as the principal of the private academy in Cohoes, New York. Arthur studied law in his spare time, preparing for admission to the New York City bar. Within two years of commencing practice, Arthur formed his own law partnership with a friend, heading west for Kansas to make his fortune. But he returned almost immediately to New York City, where two years later he married Ellen Lewis Herndon. This was a "good marriage," indeed, for the Herndons were a highly esteemed Southern aristocratic family: Ellen's mother was prominent in the society of the nation's capital, her father was a well-known ship commander who died heroically during a storm at sea, and the family had prestigious and prominent relatives. After their Episcopalian wedding ceremony, the Arthurs moved into Mrs. Herndon's expensive home on West 21st Street in Manhattan.

Very eager to pursue the main chance, Arthur had earlier launched his political career. He began inauspiciously, first by serving as a Republican polling place inspector of elections and then in 1856 as a member of the Young Man's Frémont Vigilance Committee for the 18th ward. He was soon after commissioned judge advocate of a militia brigade and three years later named "engineer-in-chief" of Governor Edwin D. Morgan's new "general staff." This was a nonpaying post that, no doubt to Arthur's pleasure, required gaudy military uniforms to be worn on state occasions. More to the point, it introduced Arthur at age 30 to a powerful man who was thereafter his friend. During the Civil War, Arthur was something less than a hero. Appointed acting assistant quartermaster general by Governor Morgan, he was soon named inspector general and then in July 1862 quartermaster general. It is possible that he used his influence to protect his wife's family's property in Virginia. He soon resigned his commission, brushed aside "the option to fight," and mapped out a private campaign to win appointment as inspector general. According to one of his friends, this was the only position Arthur would accept; it was a high enough rank and "it was a salaried position [that] permitted the incumbent to reside in New York and would not seriously interfere with [Arthur's] law practice," while leaving him "safe and comfortable." Arthur, his friend observed, "had a strong desire for money." He satisfied this desire fairly effectively, using his position as quartermaster general of New York to promote his law practice. The expeditiousness with which his firm handled war claims and drafted the necessary bills in Albany and Washington at fat fees, plus the legal services he also provided wealthy businessmen, and fortunate speculations in real estate, enabled Arthur to satisfy his sybaritic tastes. He hired a corps of servants and bought a "fine brownstone dwelling a short walk from Cyrus Field's stately home." This was fast company indeed. Arthur was elected to the city's most exclusive private clubs, socializing with J. Pierpont Morgan, and fishing and shooting with William Vanderbilt in a "Preserve in the Arcadian wilderness." At the war's end, Arthur was named to the executive committee of the great city's Republican party and in 1864 was rewarded with the post of counsel to the New York City tax commissioner at a salary of $10,000 per year. The following year, "this relatively unknown attorney" was named by the mighty Roscoe Conkling to the party's state committee.

In 1871 Arthur gained a post he had long coveted, when he was named collector of the port of New York. This was without doubt the most lucrative political plum in the nation. Until 1874, when a new law reduced the incumbent's income to $12,000 per year, Arthur was able to gross more than $50,000 annually from salary plus "moieties" or fees and fines that he shared in. Interestingly, his best biographer describes Arthur's wealth, his lofty social contacts, his comforts, his servants, his private tutors for his children, his long and expensive vacations, and his social world, marked as it was by "tiffany silver, fine carriages, and grand balls," as representing a "comfortable upper-middle class life." One wonders: what on earth then was an *upper*-class life? It is obvious that only a small fraction of one percent of the nation's families could even approximate Arthur's lifestyle, influence, and social standing.

Despite the near scandal caused by his suspension in 1877, after an investigating committee exposed wrongdoing in the customs house under his administration, Arthur survived politically to win appointments to the Republican city, central, and state committees and then in 1880 the vice-presidential nomination of the national party. Garfield's assassination in the summer of his first year in office elevated to the nation's highest office this dutiful party hack whose "specialty was . . . the science of gaining political office." No wonder a contemporary could report that "it was a common saying of that time among the men who knew him best, "'Chet' Arthur President of the United States. Good God!"

Living as a boy in a house that contained Greek and Latin classics, Milton, Shakespeare, and many works on theology, Grover Cleveland received an unusually rigorous education. At thirteen he attended the private town academy in Clinton, New York, and was one of only three youngsters who studied the *Aeneid* in the original Greek. The young Cleveland worked as a clerk in a general store in Fayetteville and on his father's death in 1853, he went to New York City for one year, working for a "pittance" at the New York Institution for the Blind. Offsetting the fact of his meager income during this period is the fact that the hardworking teenager was related to the merchant prince William E. Dodge, and was from time to time entertained in his home; moreover, Cleveland was the nephew and protégé of one of the wealthiest and most influential men in New York State, Lewis F. Allen. At eighteen Cleveland went to live with his uncle in a suburb of Buffalo, staying for a year while performing some clerical tasks for Allen. When at nineteen Cleveland went to work as a law clerk, his career path followed that of other presidents. He worked not with a humdrum firm but one, to which his uncle had introduced him, that had great prestige and served only clients who had "large interests—banks, manufacturers, shippers, and merchants." Cleveland's starting salary was small, $4.00 a week, but the experience and the contacts he made were invaluable. He was self-supporting before he was twenty. Within a year he was earning $500 plus special fees; he was admitted to the bar at twenty-two, and shortly afterward doubled his salary.

Well enough off at twenty-five to hire a substitute for $150 to fight for him in the Civil War, Cleveland observed that he could have hired a convict for nothing! He had been elected the previous year, 1862, supervisor of the second ward of Buffalo, after having served as that ward's delegate to the Democratic state convention. That later that same year he gave up his $1,000 per annum law clerkship for the position of assistant district attorney, which paid half as much, indicates that Cleveland was thinking seriously of a political career. After unsuccessfully contending for the post of district attorney, Cleveland was in 1868 named a delegate to the Democratic state convention in Albany. Simultaneously he became a partner in his own law firms, combining with men who were influential corporate lawyers. By the 1870s, when Cleveland was in his mid-thirties, he had earned a place in the "first rank among Buffalo law offices." Representing such clients as Standard Oil, the Merchants' and Traders' Bank, the Buffalo, Rochester, and Pittsburgh Railroad, and the Lehigh Valley Railroad, Cleveland was evidently liked by businessmen "because he was instinctively conservative." In the following decade, Cleveland turned down an offer that he serve as attorney to the New York Central Railroad for $15,000 per year, telling friends he did not need the money. In 1870, he accepted the seemingly modest position of sheriff of Erie County, extracting fees of more than $13,000 per year from the office and priceless political capital from his performance in it. A decade later he was named mayor of Buffalo, at a much smaller salary; at that time "it was not expected that the [officeholder] should sever all professional connections." In 1882 Cleveland was easily elected governor of New York and two years later was chosen the nation's twenty-second president.

If Cleveland, the *twenty-fourth* president—after his defeat by Benjamin Harrison in 1888 and his subsequent election in 1892—were treated as an individual distinct from Cleveland the twenty-second president, it might be noted that on the eve of his second inauguration he lived in an expensive four-story brownstone in New York City on Madison Avenue near 68th street, was a sought-after lawyer (though he was never in court), collected substantial income from consulting and from writing briefs, and had recently made a profit of almost $100,000 from the sale of property in a Washington suburb to a real estate syndicate.

Benjamin Harrison, the twenty-third president, was the grandson of William Henry Harrison, the ninth president. The

UNIVERSITY OF WALES LIBRARY SWANSEA

younger Harrison grew up on the 600-acre farm William Henry Harrison had bequeathed to his son, John Scott Harrison. Although the lifestyle of a large, hardworking agricultural family was far removed from that of William Henry Harrison's aristocratic ancestors in Virginia, it did permit large-scale entertaining and private tutors for all of John Scott Harrison's twelve children. A biographer who points up the family's recurring cash shortages notes that Benjamin Harrison's youth was an altogether happy one, unmarked by want. As a youngster of fourteen he was sent to a private academy for three years to prepare for college. Financial problems did prevent his father from sending him to Yale University or any other of the renowned "Yankee colleges" he had his heart set on; he settled instead for "the Yale of the West"—Miami University in Oxford, Ohio. After graduating in 1852 at eighteen, Harrison was sent to Cincinnati to study law with a friend of his father, Bellamy Storer, a former congressman who was both a "prominent attorney" and a man "distinguished for his social position." Admitted to the bar before he was twenty-one, Harrison found that his career quickly took off, assisted by his father's ready cash and by influential clients. The family's repute led the governor of Ohio to entrust the fledgling attorney with a legislative investigation, and led the successful William Wallace, son of a former governor and brother to the novelist Lew Wallace, to form a partnership with the twenty-two-year-old Harrison. The new firm enjoyed lucrative fees from corporate and individual clients in Philadelphia, Baltimore, Louisville, and Cincinnati. Interestingly, even as his career thrived, intermittent cash shortages compelled him to borrow money from a life-long friend, Albert Gallatin Parker, who was later to become governor of Indiana and Harrison's appointee as ambassador to Italy. In 1861 Harrison dissolved his partnership with Wallace to create a new law firm that was soon in the "front rank among Indianapolis law offices." Harrison was very popular with business clients largely because, like Cleveland, he was "instinctively conservative" in his advice. Harrison enrolled in July 1862 as a second lieutenant to enlist volunteers for a new regiment. During the next two years he saw heavy action, attaining the rank of brigadier general. At the end of the war, he returned to his law practice. His income, when supplemented by the salary he earned as a reporter of the supreme court of Indiana, soon passed $10,000 per year.

A politically ambitious man, Harrison, as early as 1857 when he was twenty-four, had for one full year forsaken private income in order to accept an elective post as city attorney of Indianapolis for a mere $400 a year. As his biographer observes, "there is no question that at this period of his life he aspired to political prominence." Frankly conceding that he owed his appointment to his father's influence and to his own importuning of the support of important men, Harrison was also named commissioner of the court of claims. Soon after he was named secretary to the Indiana Republican central committee and offered candidacy for the state legislature. His private career outshone his public, for in 1872 he failed to garner the Republican nomination for governor and four years later, when he did win it, he lost the election. After being named by President Hayes in 1879 to the Mississippi River Commission, Harrison was two years later elected by the Indiana legislature to the U.S. Senate. One year after his Senate term was completed, Harrison won the Republican nomination for the presidency and, despite his failure to win a majority of the popular votes, was elected.

As a grown man, William McKinley was to say of his boyhood days that they were "pure luxury," never equaled in his later experience. He was no doubt speaking of emotional rather than material luxury, for his father's management of a furnace in Niles, Ohio, hardly afforded the family a sybaritic existence. McKinley was sent to a private academy in Poland, Ohio, before entering Allegheny College in Meadville, Ohio, in 1860. The following year he volunteered for the Ohio infantry, serving under Col. Rutherford B. Hayes. Before the war ended, McKinley saw action and was promoted to the brevet commission of major. After the war he began to read for the law with a Youngstown law firm, before enrolling in 1866 in the Albany, New York, law school. As a lawyer, McKinley, according to his most thorough biographer, "had none of the shrewd and imaginative drive for profit that makes for business success," since "the accumulation of wealth held no interest for him at all." He did indeed do well but his ambition centered on political goals rather than great financial gains. At one point in his career, after he had been elected to Congress, McKinley turned down a large western railroad's offer of an annual salary of more than $25,000, so that he might remain in an office paying less than one quarter that sum. He preferred, he said, to stay with work he was familiar with and which permitted him to serve the country "a little." His marriage to Ida Paxton, daughter of an Ohio banker, abetted his rise (although the fact that shortly after marriage she was invalided did strain the family's financial resources).

After thriving, if modestly, in the decade after the war's end through the success of his law practice and his shrewd investments in Ohio real estate and industry, McKinley at age 42 decided to put law aside for politics. In the "era of the bloody shirt," a lawyer who was a combat veteran of the Civil War from the magic state of Ohio and who enjoyed a reputation as a conservative businessman of sound beliefs had some reason to hope for a career in national politics. McKinley was elected to Congress in 1876, serving in the House almost without interruption until 1891. As chairman of the Ways and Means Committee of the House, in 1890 he helped push through the McKinley tariff, beloved of protectionists. His general comportment as congressman and his prospects won him what was to be invaluable special attention and support from the rich and influential businessman, Mark Hanna. In 1892 McKinley was elected to the first of his two terms as governor of Ohio and in 1896 he won the Republican party's presidential nomination. Contributing to McKinley's rise was his politic penchant for joining and actively participating in the affairs of a wide variety of organizations—diverse Civil War veterans groups, the Masons, the Knights of the Temple, the Knights of Pythias, the YMCA, the Methodist church, and, of course, the Republican party.

A biographer writes that during Theodore Roosevelt's childhood, "there was money enough for all necessary comforts of life." These words are understatement. When young Roosevelt was believed to need additional exercise in order to maintain his health, his father contracted for a private gymnasium to be built on the second floor of the family's elegantly furnished town house in New York City. Before TR was fourteen, he more than once accompanied his family on the Grand Tour, spending months absorbing the sights and culture of London, Rome, Paris, Versailles, and other great cities on the Continent. Since his parents "did not wish to see their children 'coarsened' by public schools," he received his education at the hands of private tutors and at the finest prep schools, before enrolling at Harvard in 1876 at seventeen. At Harvard he belonged to the most exclusive clubs, in the company of the Van Rensselaers of New York and the Codmans, Minots, and Saltonstalls of Massachusetts, as befit a child of the old Dutch elite of New York and the Georgia aristocracy. An insight into both his intelligence and his snobbishness while he attended Harvard is afforded by one of his letters to his sister, Bamie. "I stand 19th in the class, which began with 230 fellows. . . . Only one gentleman stands ahead of me." At college, he spent thousands of dollars on clothes and club dues, amounts that, according to a recent biographer, "the average American family could have lived on for six years." While at Harvard, he met, fell in love with, and married Alice Lee, whose family tree contained Cabots, Saltonstalls, and Higginsons, among other eminences. (Tragedy struck in 1884—his wife and his mother died on the same day. Two years later Roosevelt married a playmate of his youth, Edith Carow, of a long-prestigious New York family.) After graduating from Harvard, Roosevelt enrolled at Columbia University Law School but he never completed his courses.

When his father died in 1878, TR inherited $125,000, from which he derived an income of between $7,500 and $10,000 a year, a princely sum for that time, which made it unnecessary for Roosevelt to work for a living. (On slightly more than half that income, President Eliot of Harvard "kept a comfortable home, entertained, owned a summer house, a boat, and put his own two sons through Harvard.") Young Roosevelt supplemented his inheritance with returns from investments in railroads, banks, and ranches. That he was subsequently "mildly embarrassed" for funds from time to time was due not to want in the ordinary sense of the term but rather to his recklessness in "personal financial matters." In every sense of the term, he could afford to be reckless. Once, when he had only $10,000 in the bank to cover his investment of $20,000 in G. P. Putnam's, the publishers, he simply turned to his uncle, the banker James A. Roosevelt, who arranged matters satisfactorily. When, as a young man, he invested many tens of thousands of dollars in the cattle business and the investment turned out a fiasco, he could cheerfully brush off the loss, finding compensation—of the nonfinancial sort—in "dividends" that were intangible. Even before his twenty-second birthday, he began buying property at Oyster Bay, eventually paying $30,000 for 155 hilltop acres he acquired there. Two years later he agreed to pay carpenters almost $17,000 to begin building the house that had been designed by a major architectural firm. His imposing eight-fireplace structure at Sagamore Hill, looked after by ten servants, was built as a summer resort "cottage." When he was twenty-five this "gentleman cowboy" owned two ranches and was shortly to organize a polo club among his Long Island friends. He soon acquired too a town house on Madison Avenue in New York City. When Roosevelt was later to write of his post-Harvard years that he "had enough to get bread" but not enough "to provide butter and jam," he was merely indulging a momentary penchant for understatement.

On graduating from Harvard, Roosevelt shocked his friends by evincing an interest in public service. For this young snob believed, as he told a reporter, that "the respected, educated, refined young men of this city should have more weight in public matters." His friends thought such service would "soil the linen of a gentleman." But, as he told them, he "intended to be one of the governing class." That he indeed became one, going on to truly striking achievements as a political leader, was due in part, no doubt, to his ability and his personality. But it is also true that he was able to commence such a career primarily because of his wealth and family eminence. When the young law student became active in the 21st District Republican Club of New York City, he had no trouble being nominated for and winning a seat in the state assembly and, shortly after, gaining a strategic committee membership entirely because of his uncle Robert Barnhill Roosevelt's influence with top leaders of the Democratic party in the state.

For all the questions some of TR's younger elite friends may have had about the propriety of participating in politics, the adult leaders of New York's upper crust entertained no such doubts. His decision was strongly backed by Joseph Choate, J. Pierpont Morgan, and Elihu Root, among others, and his turn to politics was launched by a testimonial dinner at Delmonico's thrown for him by three hundred social and financial leaders wearing white tie and tails. An assemblyman's salary of $1200 a year may have been an inducement to some plebeian types but it had slight meaning to TR. Reelected twice, he became minority leader of the assembly before deciding in 1884 to go west for one season because he "had nothing else to do." On his return, he ran for mayor of New York City, unsuccessfully, and in 1889 he was appointed to the United States Civil Service Commission. The $3500 salary was hardly the important enticement to this young man, who was not above accepting the most mundane posts of government in his climb toward the top. His appointment to the New York City police board in 1895 and his brilliant exploitation of this post were milestones in his political career. In 1897 he was named assistant secretary of the Navy. He resigned the following year, when the Spanish-American War broke out. This onetime captain of the New York National Guard now became lieutenant colonel of the regiment of "Rough Riders." The instant war hero was elected governor of New York in 1898. Two years later he was nominated by the Republican party to be McKinley's running mate and was thus the political heir to the presidency in 1901 on the assassination of McKinley.

Not to be omitted from an account of Roosevelt's career are the many books he wrote on history and on his own experiences in the west. A sympathetic early biographer observed that they were hastily done, superficial studies that "reflect small credit on Roosevelt as a historian." Whatever else he may have been, Theodore Roosevelt was no great thinker. Possessed of insatiable curiosity about all manner of things, Roosevelt was able to indulge his diverse interests primarily because of the wealth and position afforded by his eminent family.

In 1908, just before William Howard Taft, Theodore Roosevelt's personal choice, was selected for the Republican presidential nomination, the famous newspaperman William Allen White asked Taft: "Where [do] you get your political pull?" According to an early biographer, Taft replied "at some length and with charming candor." He explained his political success by his hard work and his personality, among other things, but he was frank enough to say that he owed it, first of all, to his "father's prominence." Taft provides yet another example of a president who clearly had superlative talents but who had the opportunity to display them primarily because of inherited advantages not available to most Americans. If, as a young man, Taft was not sent to Cincinnati's best and most exclusive private schools, it was because of his father's evident belief in the "virtue of public education." In accord with a family plan conceived during his infancy, Taft attended Yale, where he was an outstanding student. A biographer finds it necessary to explain at some length why Taft did not attend law school at Yale or another prestigious eastern institution. Cincinnati Law School was, however, one of the oldest in the nation and evidently comported with his father's plan that his son attend a professional school near home. Whatever law school Taft attended, he was a young man of "assured position."

After completing law school, Taft turned down a well-paying job in journalism in order to do the part-time work in court hearings that he felt would add significantly to his legal knowledge. Appointed in 1880 at age 23 to the post of assistant prosecutor of Hamilton County, Ohio, Taft began what was to be an almost unbroken career of public service, culminating a third of a century later in his occupancy of the White House. Although he quickly formed a partnership with his father's former associate Major Harlan Page Lloyd, Taft remained in private law practice for only two years. Since money was neither problem nor issue to him, he could focus his attention on realizing his political ambitions. These, it turned out, were indeed lofty, leading him, at one stage, to reject mere appointments to the United States Supreme Court—he wanted to be chief justice. When he married Helen Herron in 1886, he was able to build an impressive house in a scenic area on a large lot given by his father-in-law. His biographers say little or nothing about the inheritance left Taft on his father's death in 1891. As one of them observes, although Taft in the years following liked to talk about the "happiness of poverty," he was evidently a substantial provider who owned, among other properties, a lovely summer place on the St. Lawrence River. It is true that the salary Taft received even for such a prestigious position as secretary of war was not lavish. But the more than $8,000 per year that was remitted to Taft by his "generous" brother Charles, provided "money enough for champagne." After holding a series of modest political positions in the Cincinnati area, Taft at twenty-nine was named to the superior court and two years later, in 1889, named solicitor general of the United States. In 1892 he was made a judge for the federal court of appeals. During the eight years in which he held this position, he served too as dean of the Cincinnati Law School. Promised subsequent promotion of his judicial career if he accepted the new post, Taft in 1900 consented to be McKinley's choice for commissioner and then civil governor of the Philippine Islands. Two years later he was sent on a special mission to the Vatican before being named secretary of war by Roosevelt in 1904. In 1908 he lived up to the words he had earlier written a friend, in which, while noting that his chief ambition lay in the judiciary rather than the executive, Taft presumed that "there are very few men who would refuse to accept the nomination of the Republican party for the presidency, and [he was] not an exception."

Woodrow Wilson was born in a "manse" in Staunton, Virginia, an imposing, stately structure whose two-story portico reminds one architectural historian of Jefferson's first Monticello home. Wilson's father, although very prestigious, was not very rich. The family's wealth was substantially enhanced, however, by the "considerable sum of money" left Mrs. Wilson by her wealthy bachelor brother during Woodrow Wilson's boyhood. The family was thus able to build one of the finest houses in Columbia, South Carolina, where the elder Wilson was both pastor of the first Presbyterian Church and a professor at the theological seminary. Wilson enrolled at Davidson College in 1873 and, after leaving at the end of the first year because of illness, entered Princeton in 1875. On graduating, he entered the University of Virginia Law School but once again was forced to withdraw because of a breakdown of his health. After winning his degree in 1882 and gaining admission to the Georgia bar, Wilson decided to forsake law for an academic life devoted to teaching and scholarly publication in history and political science. During his brief legal career, his only client was his mother. Wilson enrolled at Johns Hopkins University in 1883, earning his Ph.D. degree in political science in 1886. By that time he had become a professor of history at the new Bryn Mawr College, married Ellen Louise Axson, daughter of his father's colleague and friend, and published an unusually significant first book, *Congressional Government.* After teaching for two years at Wesleyan in Middletown, Connecticut, Wilson in 1890 returned to Princeton—this time as professor of jurisprudence and political economy—to launch a remarkably successful career at that institution. By the time he was named president of Princeton in 1902, he had established a great reputation as a scholar. His five-volume *History of the American People,* completed that year, earned him substantial income as well as scholarly acclaim, culminating a decade in which he three times had been offered and three times refused the presidency of the University of Virginia.

This was one scholar whose renown was not confined to academic circles. Wilson's leadership in the campaign to liberalize Princeton and his much-publicized assault on the university's restrictive eating clubs earned him a national reputation and aroused the interest of New Jersey Democrats in this man known to harbor political ambitions. After earlier considering and ultimately rejecting a nomination for the U.S. Senate, Wilson in 1910 accepted the Democratic nomination for governor of New Jersey. As he wrote a friend at the time, the "question of my nomination for the governorship is the mere preliminary of a plan to nominate me in 1912 for the presidency." The plan succeeded. Despite receiving no more than forty-two percent of the popular vote, Wilson was elected, benefiting from the decision of Theodore Roosevelt to contest the candidacy of Taft, a man Roosevelt now considered a renegade to the reform principles he held dear.

As a youngster growing up in the small Ohio communities of Blooming Grove and Caledonia (population 700), Warren G. Harding did the chores associated with boyhood in semirural towns. He milked cows, curried horses, worked in the fields, painted barns, and made bricks and brooms, among other jobs. But since his father was a doctor for much of this period, young Harding worked not because of family need but because work of the sort he did was the norm for children even of well-to-do families. When at age 10 he worked as a printer's "devil," it was in the offices of the newspaper his father had recently bought, the *Caledonian Argus.* Harding entered Iberia College as a stripling and graduated in 1882 at age 16. Tuition at this tiny institution with a faculty of three was $7 a term. (The significance of a college such as this as index to a young man's social and economic standing was not its expensiveness but rather the fact that his family was in a position to free him from the necessity of working for income.) After graduating, Harding, who had exhibited neither noteworthy intellect nor special aptitudes, wandered from one humdrum activity to another, working for a while as grade school teacher, cornet player and later manager of the Marion, Ohio band, insurance agent, manager and second-string first baseman on the town's baseball team, and dabbling at some law books that had been picked up by his father.

It tells something of the standards of a small town newspaper of the time, on the one hand, and the power of nepotism, on the other, that at age 18 this unimpressive young man could become editor of the Marion *Daily Star,* a paper in which his father had recently bought a half-interest. Working too as an "odd job reporter" for the Marion *Mirror,* Harding in less than a year became a one-third owner of the *Star* by investing $100, as did two of his friends. He quickly won an additional one-third share in a poker game. It is doubtless a sign of Harding's ability that, before he was twenty, his newspaper had progressed from a laughingstock to the paper with a circulation twice as large as the town's other two newspapers. Over the next five years the *Star* became as successful as any small town journal in the state, aided in part by Harding's occasional editorials but even more by his knack for drumming up trade and charming people with what evidently only seemed idle talk. In 1891 at twenty-five Harding married Florence Mabel Kling, daughter of Marion's richest businessman. She was five years older than Harding; eleven years earlier, while pregnant, she had contracted what turned out to be a short-lived marriage that led to a break with her father. Although Amos Kling eventually became reconciled both to his daughter and to her new husband, his initial disposition toward Harding was less than pleasant. For when he met his son-in-law on the street, he "called him a nigger, and threatened to blow his head off." Kling initiated a series of suits designed to bring ruin both to Harding and his father, but these attacks came to naught and Harding thrived, in part because of the orderly system introduced into the *Star*'s operations by its new circulation manager, Florence Mabel Kling Harding.

As the town of Marion grew by the turn of the century into a city of almost 20,000, its leading newspaper grew, too, making its editor and publisher Warren G. Harding rich in the process. Beloved of businessmen because his journal unfailingly boosted business in general and business in Ohio in particular, Harding invested heavily and profitably in oil, gas, iron, and engineering firms. Harding had been able even at age 25 to build a large, impressive, and expensive house in a swank neighborhood for his new bride. In subsequent decades, Harding added a "fine library" to his home, traveled widely and often, and enjoyed an increasingly opulent lifestyle in company with the town's elite. Always a joiner, the mature Harding belonged to Marion's most prestigious clubs and its most influential voluntary associations; he sat as director on the boards of its leading corporations. Combining good looks that, in their "virile maleness," were particularly attractive to women, wealth, business acumen, and a personality and ideology that appealed to businessmen, Harding had little difficulty in making a place for himself in the political world.

Blessed with a resonant voice and a gift for cliché that complemented his other assets, Harding, after starting out at twenty-two as delegate to the Republican state convention, within five years became the leader of Marion's young Republicans, as his newspaper became their chief instrument. Elected and reelected to the state senate at the turn of the century, Harding was in 1903 elected lieutenant governor of Ohio. After losing a close race for governor in 1910, Harding was four years later elected a U.S. senator. Although his Senate record was abysmal, whether for attendance or performance, this pleasant, ideologically reliable man was nominated by the Republican party for the highest office in 1920, owing his choice not least to his physical appearance. For as an influential man, a power in Ohio politics, said to himself on first meeting Harding: "What a great-looking president he'd make!" And who can deny that he indeed turned out to be a "great-looking president"?

In his autobiography, Coolidge wrote that he grew up in a household in which, "whatever was needed never failed to be provided." At thirteen Coolidge left home to go to the Black River Academy in Ludlow, Vermont, a private school attended by very few boys from his hometown. At school Coolidge belonged to the select circle within a select circle that studied the classical course given as preparation for college. His father bore the annual cost of about $150. On completing his course, Coolidge went to Amherst College, joining a student body made up primarily of sons of professional men. Although William Allen White has described Coolidge's father variously as "squire," "land-owner aristocrat," and member of the "ruling classes," and Coolidge himself described his father as a great success, the fact remains that he evidently lacked the financial resources to send his son to law school. Instead Coolidge read for the law and in the tradition of earlier lawyer-presidents, did so with men of renown, substance, and influence in their Northampton community. Their invitation to him was extended just after he had asked to read with the former governor of Vermont, William P. Dillingham, a man his father knew. Shortly after being admitted to the Massachusetts bar in 1897 at twenty-five, Coolidge entered into private practice and by his second year was making $1400 or three times as much as he did during his first year. He had good business clients and as city solicitor he made another $600 a year in a post that complemented rather than interfered with his private practice. In 1905 at thirty-three, he married Grace Anna Goodhue, a graduate of the University of Vermont, who a few years earlier had come to teach in Northampton. After renting what Coolidge called a "very comfortable house that needed but one maid," the couple bought a new home after being married one year and they managed to save a good deal of money.

Well before marriage, Coolidge had exhibited an interest in politics—Republican party politics—and from age 25 on he was continually engaged in it at one level or another. His start was promoted by the senior partners in his law firm, Henry P. Field and John C. Hammond, who used his services in their own successful campaigns for mayor and district attorney respectively. They recruited Coolidge into the "lower ranks of Northampton's Republican hierarchy." Serving at first as a member of Northampton's Republican city committee and as a member of the city's common council, a nonpaying post, Coolidge was then for three years city solicitor and in 1903 appointed temporary "clerk of the courts" for Hampshire County at $2300 per year. After serving two terms in the state's lower house, Coolidge was at thirty-seven elected mayor of Northampton, a position which did not "interfere seriously" with his private practice.

According to Coolidge, he did not plan for a career in politics; it "just came." Whatever his motives, his political career now began to thrive. After serving as mayor for one year, he was elected to the state senate and reelected three times. In 1914 he was selected president of the body. The following year he began the first of three terms as lieutenant governor of Massachusetts. After becoming governor of the state in 1918, Coolidge gave up his private law practice. His path to the national party's nomination for the vice-presidency was dramatically cleared for him by the Boston police strike in 1919. His telegram to Samuel Gompers, president of the American Federation of Labor, on September 4 won him almost immediate acclaim. The man who wrote that "there is no right to strike against the public safety by anybody, anywhere, anytime," was in 1920 named to the second spot on the Republican party national ticket and on Harding's death in 1923 rose to the very top.

A year after his mother's death had left him an orphan at ten, Herbert Hoover went to live with his maternal uncle, Dr. Henry J. Minthorn, a doctor who was in the land business in Oregon. As a teenager, Hoover worked in his uncle's office, went to the private academy his uncle superintended, and took math courses evenings at a local business school. At seventeen, in 1891, he enrolled at Stanford University where, interestingly, in view of his later reputation, he became involved in campus politics on the "progressive" and "populist" side against the so-called "snob element." Majoring in and evidently mastering geology and mining more than compensated for his mediocre grades in languages and other subjects. Working as an office clerk and newspaper boy in addition to starting a laundry service during his freshman year, the enterprising youngster also became the part-time secretary of a professor, Dr. John Branner, who happened to be one of the nation's leading geologists. Branner helped get him a summer job with the geological survey of Arkansas at the end of his first year at Stanford and a job with the U.S. geological survey for each of the next two summers. After graduation, Hoover worked for a short time as a miner, first as an underground "mucker" and then as a helper on a drill, before making what turned out to be a fortunate connection with the firm of the mining expert Louis Janin. After first working as a copyist or clerk, Hoover was soon being sent out to survey mines, among other assignments. One good thing swiftly led to another. Within two years, Hoover landed a well-paying post with a large corporation in Australia. Hoover invested part of his $10,000-a-year salary in a mine that was a bonanza of gold production and he attained an interest in the firm. At twenty-five, just before he went off to Peking on a job that paid $20,000 a year plus expenses, Hoover married Lou Henry, the daughter of a Monterey, California bank president, a young woman he had first met while attending Stanford. A biographer writes that the couple enjoyed "top-shelf social status." Two years later Hoover accepted a junior partnership with Bewick, Moreing and Company, a large London firm specializing in the management of other people's properties and in technical advising. Although there were other men who were more expert technically than Hoover, his evident organizing ability and business acumen enabled him to be in the position of employing such men.

By the outbreak of World War I, when Hoover was forty, he was a millionaire several times over. He and his wife lived in elegant and spacious quarters in Kensington Gardens, regularly entertaining well-known politicians and financiers as well as celebrities from other fields. He was now in a position to forsake direct involvement in business for public service. That money was neither a problem nor a consideration in his subsequent behavior is clear from the fact that in 1921 he could turn down an offer of a full partnership and a guaranteed annual income of more than one-half million dollars with the Guggenheim brothers, owners of the largest mining and metallurgical company in the world, in order to be secretary of commerce in the Harding cabinet at $15,000 per year. Hoover earned public renown for his performance as head of the commission for relief in Belgium, a nonpaying job, and then as food "czar" or head of the American Food Administration. He followed these assignments by heading the Allied Food Council and then, after the war, by supervising several agencies that were responsible for relief in Europe. In 1919 he was named a member of the American delegation to the Paris Peace Conference. After serving in the commerce department through the Harding and Coolidge administrations, Hoover won the Republican presidential nomination in 1928.

Franklin D. Roosevelt's youth and early adult career were colored above all by the wealth, comfort, educational advantages, and the lofty social standing conferred on him by his aristocratic family. Born and raised on the family's lavish Hudson River estage, young Roosevelt regularly spent several months abroad, had private tutors, hunted and rode to the hounds, and led a sheltered existence in which, according to a respected biographer, "few of the worries of American life of the '80s and '90s intruded beyond the gates of Hyde Park." Summers would be spent amidst the "invigorating sea air and the congenial social life" on the Canadian island of Campobello, where the family had built a home on four acres of land. With other children from "social register families," Roosevelt attended the exclusive Groton school and when at Harvard he moved in the rarefied sphere of aristocrats, dating and squiring at dances young women of the "best" Massachusetts families—Sohiers, Lymans, and Quincys. Weekends at college might be spent duckhunting at a rich friend's place in Newburyport. Much more the social lion than a bookish grind, Roosevelt did attend Columbia University Law School after graduating from Harvard but he never bothered to complete his courses or earn his law degree. This of course in no way interfered with his landing a post with a Wall Street law firm that numbered Standard Oil of New Jersey and the American Tobacco Company among its clients. Income was not princely but more to the point, it was no issue to this young man who is said to have had "little interest in making additional money, especially if the means of making it were dull." After graduating from Harvard he married his cousin Eleanor Roosevelt, who was a niece of Theodore Roosevelt. Her family tree on the maternal side was no less lustrous than FDR's. While the young couple were spending their honeymoon traveling in Europe, Roosevelt cabled his mother from Venice, asking if she cared to have the furniture, woodwork, and mosaic floors from an old palace, all of which he could get for a mere $60,000. In London the newlyweds paid $1,000 a day for the royal suite in Brown's Hotel. In addition to their own summer cottage next to Sara Roosevelt's on Campobello, Franklin and Eleanor maintained a six-story home and servants in New York City. Young Roosevelt was a member of the Hudson-Fulton Celebration Commission and Hyde Park fire engine companies, a director of the First National Bank of Poughkeepsie, vice-commodore of the Hudson River Ice Club, vestryman in St. James Episcopal Church, and a member of the New York Yacht Club and the Knickerbocker Club. Rather than lawyer and breadwinner, his "favored roles [were] Hudson River gentleman, yachtsman, philatelist, and naval historian."

When at twenty-eight Roosevelt decided to enter politics, he had no difficulty, given his wealth, social standing, and fine appearance, in winning a nomination to the New York state assembly. He won a close election in 1910 and two years later an almost equally close race for reelection. A Democrat by family tradition, he was named assistant secretary of the navy by President Wilson in 1913, a position he held until 1920. That year he was nominated for the vice-presidency by the Democratic party but he was submerged in the Harding landslide. Punctuating his ten-year career of public service by a vacation spent duckhunting in Louisiana, Roosevelt returned to private life in New York City, where he soon reestablished himself as a successful lawyer and businessman—although he gave relatively little time and energy to these mundane pursuits. He was above all a social activist and humanitarian, a role that comported well with what were obviously the great political ambitions and prospects of this attractive and glamorous man. After a testimonial dinner (launching his new career as financier) tendered him at Delmonico's by some of the nation's leading financiers, Roosevelt assumed his duties as vice-president in charge of the New York Office of the Fidelity and Deposit Company of Maryland, the nation's third-largest surety bonding company. The salary in this position, which a rich friend had lined up for him, was $25,000 per year. Roosevelt spent no more than a few mornings a week performing his tasks as—in his phrase—one of the "younger capitalists," reserving his afternoons for his involvement first in one prestigious law partnership and then another. Although he may not have had to work hard as a capitalist, he represented a most fruitful addition to his firm, since his contacts were many and the contracts his name attracted were lucrative. During the 1920s, the young lawyer-capitalist had far-flung investments in banks, investment companies, bond corporations, trust companies, oil companies, airlines, merchandising corporations, a lobster company, and an automatic camera company; he also donated $200,000 to the Warm Springs Foundation, and served without pay as president of the American Construction Council.

In the best aristocratic tradition of noblesse oblige, he managed too to contribute to or participate in what a biographer calls "an astonishing variety and quantity of political, charitable, and social activities." He was, among other things, "one of the overseers of Harvard, director of the Seaman's Church Institute, President of the Navy Club, chairman of the fund-raising committee for Lighthouses for the Blind, chairman of the Greater New York Committee of the Boy Scouts of America, . . . a member of the Near East Relief Commission, the Council of the American Geographic Society, and the executive committee of the National Civic Federation." As party man, his loyal support of Al Smith, the Democratic presidential candidate in 1928, was rewarded by the nomination of Roosevelt that year for governor of New York. After winning a close race, his performance in that strategic office earned him a decisive victory in 1930 and nomination to the nation's highest office in 1932.

As a boy Harry Truman grew up on the large Missouri farm operated by his father. Later he would say that some of his "happiest and most pleasant recollections" were of playing as a child on the 600-acre Young farm in Jackson County and later at "the big new house" in Independence that was a magnet to youngsters "for blocks around." Although the elder Truman often did well, earning what was for the late-nineteenth century the lavish net income of $15,000 per year, the younger Truman did not attend college. After graduating from high school at age 17 in 1901, Truman worked as a railroad timekeeper, as assistant to a contractor (during which time he lived in hobo camps), as a clerk in the Kansas City *Star* mailroom, and first as a clerk and then as a bookkeeper in several banks. After his family had inherited an estate valued at $150,000 from Louisa Young, Truman at twenty-two moved into his grandfather's house and ran the family farm for a period he estimates at from "ten to twelve years." At the end of this period, he invested $5,000 in an oil drilling firm, having just inherited part of his grandfather's farm. When the United States entered the war in 1917, Truman, who had twelve years earlier joined the national guard, enlisted as a junior lieutenant in the field artillery; he was subsequently twice promoted and saw active service in France. On returning to civilian life at age 35, he married Elizabeth (Bess) Virginia Wallace, whose family were among the "aristocracy" of Independence, Missouri. Her grandfather George Gates was the founder of a very successful flour milling company and a "pillar of the Independence social set." In partnership with his friend Eddie Jacobson, Truman now invested $15,000 in a men's furnishing goods store in Kansas City. Although the store did very well for a while, it failed in less than two years because of what Truman was convinced were the harmful economic policies of the Republican administration in Washington. Truman narrowly avoided bankruptcy. Even before he suffered this business disappointment, Truman had entered politics.

Asked in 1921 if he would accept nomination as candidate for the administrative, not judicial, office of judge for the county court of the eastern district, Truman accepted the following year, spurred on by his business failure. During his tenure he enrolled in courses at the Kansas City Law School. After he was defeated for reelection in 1924, Truman worked the next year and a half with the Automobile Club of Kansas City, earning what he called "substantial income." Truman's mining investments did not pan out and according to his daughter Margaret, the haberdashery store misadventure cost him almost $30,000. Yet he evidently had it to lose. Truman himself reports that a farm he bought in the early 1920s for just under $15,000 was actually worth "considerably more than that figure." Margaret Truman remembers that as a child she burst into tears of disappointment at the Christmas present he bought her—a baby grand piano. In 1926, with the support of the Pendergast machine, Truman was elected presiding judge of the county court, at $6,000 per year. After holding the position for eight years, he was elected in 1934 to the U.S. Senate, just after he had been "maneuvered out of" running for Congress, at least according to his own recollection. Reelected to the Senate in 1940, he did not complete his term, for in 1944 party chieftains substituted him for Henry A. Wallace as FDR's running mate on the Democratic ticket. In view of Roosevelt's declining health, it was hardly surprising that Truman ascended to the chief executive's office shortly after Roosevelt's term began.

Since Dwight Eisenhower's adult years were spent largely in

the army, an account of his prepresidential career can be brief. Born in Denison, Texas, and raised in Abilene, Kansas, first in a small cottage and then in an ample house set on three acres, which a relative had sold his father at a bargain price, Eisenhower had a happy youth. Working on the family farm during his boyhood years and in his uncle's creamery while he went to high school, Eisenhower became night foreman of the plant on his graduation at nineteen from Abilene High School. Two years later he began what was to be more than a third of a century of continuous military service by enrolling in West Point. He graduated in 1915 and the next year at age 25 he married Mamie Geneva Doud. As a biographer observes, there was a vast difference "in economic and social status" between the Douds and Eisenhowers. Arriving in Guilford, Connecticut, from Surrey in 1639, where they evidently were part of the English aristocracy, Mamie's family on both sides had prospered here and her father had made a fortune in business. Small wonder that her parents pointed out that a "second lieutenant's pay could not support her in the style to which she was accustomed." Eisenhower was promoted to lieutenant on July 1, 1916, his wedding day, but it is doubtful that his bride's parents were much impressed.

Eisenhower's subsequent military career is of course the stuff of legend. After a tour of duty in San Antonio, he was over the next five years promoted several times until he was made lieutenant colonel, only to have the rank reduced to the permanent rank of captain in "a shrinking army" and then three days later to be raised again, this time to major. After serving in Panama during the 1920s, Eisenhower at the end of the decade was made assistant executive in the office of the assistant secretary of war. During the 1930s he turned down an offer of between $15,000 and $20,000 a year to be the military expert for a large newspaper chain. The outbreak of World War II gave him his great chance and, as the world knows, he proved more than equal to it. In November, 1940, he was named chief of staff of the 3rd Division, four months later promoted to the temporary rank of full colonel, and a half year after that rewarded for his work as the chief of staff by promotion to the temporary rank of brigadier general. After Pearl Harbor his star rose meteorically. Named major general and assistant chief of staff in charge of war plans, in less than two years he was raised to commander of the European theatre, the temporary rank of general, and in November, 1943, Supreme Commander of the Allied Expeditionary Forces. After D-Day in June, 1944, and V-E Day eleven months later, Eisenhower's popularity was such that he could have had nomination to the highest office by merely letting it be known that he was willing. He chose to wait seven years. Prodded by Thomas J. Watson of IBM, Eisenhower announced in the summer of 1947 that he would soon replace Nicholas Murray Butler as president of Columbia University. Eisenhower was permitted by special act of Congress to pocket most of the more than half-million dollars he earned from his book recounting his wartime experiences, *Crusade in Europe.* But of course his wealth paled in comparison to the fortunes of the corporate movers and shakers who almost alone were his circle in the years after the war, whether on the golf course, at the bridge table, or at informal occasions. At the beginning of 1951 Eisenhower returned to active duty as the Supreme Commander of the Allied Powers in Europe and in 1952 finally let the country in on his party preference by accepting the Republican nomination for the presidency.

Born the year of America's entry into the first world war, John F. Kennedy grew up in luxurious circumstances unclouded by money worries. A trust fund established during the future president's childhood assured the material ease of all of Joseph P. Kennedy's children, and subsequent additions to the fund earmarked more than ten million dollars for each of them. The youngsters were looked after by domestic servants, a nurse, and a governess in their large house in Brookline. During Jack's youth, his father bought an impressive house in Bronxville on a four-acre estate, a large summer house containing fifteen rooms and nine baths in the Cape Cod village of Hyannis Port, and, for wintering, a house in Palm Beach that Addison Mizener had designed for Rodman Wanamaker. After first attending exclusive Catholic prep schools in New Milford, Connecticut, JFK was sent to the more select Episcopalian prep school, Choate, in Wallingford, Connecticut.

On graduating from Choate in 1935 at eighteen, Kennedy spent a summer at the London School of Economics before enrolling at Princeton. After illness compelled him to leave part way through his freshman year, Kennedy enrolled at Harvard the following year. Graduating in 1940, Kennedy's senior thesis was subsequently published under the title, *Why England Slept.* After attending the Stanford University Business School for half a year, Kennedy was in 1941 appointed an ensign in the U.S. Navy. After Pearl Harbor he saw action in the South Pacific, earning a Purple Heart and the Navy and Marine Corps medal for his role in saving members of his crew after the patrol boat under his command, PT-109, had been sunk by a Japanese destroyer. After the war, Kennedy worked for a short time as a reporter for the Hearst press. A politically ambitious son of an ambitious father, Kennedy in 1946 commenced his political career by running for the House of Representatives. Aided by expenditures that have been estimated at between $50,000 and $250,000, but that in any case were far greater than the sum his opponents spent in the primary and the election, Kennedy won as he did again in 1948 and 1950. When in 1952 he defeated the Republican candidate for the U.S. Senate, the incumbent Henry Cabot Lodge, Jr., Kennedy's campaign expenditure of more than a half-million dollars was from eight to ten times as much as Lodge spent.

Shortly after his election to the Senate, Kennedy married Jacqueline Lee Bouvier. The marriage was socially lustrous, for the Bouviers commanded loftier social status than the Kennedys, belonging as the bride's family did to what one biographer calls "America's untitled aristocracy." (It is of course nothing more than coincidence but, doing research on the backgrounds and social interconnections of elite families of 150 years ago, I was struck by the fact that John Bouvier, a prestigious lawyer in Philadelphia during the Jacksonian era, was the "legal protégé" of the equally eminent John Kennedy!) When her parents divorced, Jackie's mother married Hugh Auchincloss, a rich Washington businessman and descendant of a long-eminent line. The "deb of the year" in 1948 when she "came out" in parties in New York and Newport, Miss Bouvier married the future president at an elaborate wedding in Newport in 1953. While still in his first term as senator, Kennedy tried unsuccessfully to win the Democratic vice-presidential nomination in 1956. He had much better luck when he interrupted his second senatorial term after he had easily won reelection in 1956. He now set his sights on the presidency. Beneficiary of a "publicity buildup unprecedented in United States political history," and vast expenditures that left his rivals far in the wake—his father told a friend, "we're going to sell Jack like soap flakes!"—Kennedy won the Democratic nomination and then defeated Richard M. Nixon in the dramatically close election of 1960.

Lyndon Johnson's boyhood years were marked by the comforts and advantages resulting from his father's success in farming, cattle dealing, business, property accumulation, speculation, and state politics. But after the bottom dropped out of the cotton market in 1921, when the future president was thirteen, Sam Johnson, Jr., found himself first overextended and then ruined. Until the end of his life, sixteen years later, he never did pull himself out of debt and the family's circumstances changed drastically for the worse. Interestingly, he was nevertheless elected to the state legislature during this dark period and, for all the family's near-poverty, the aura and prestige of having been *someone* never did forsake Sam Johnson completely. As the family was compelled to give up its ample house for more modest quarters by the Pedernales, the young LBJ was removed from one school to another. After graduating from Johnson City High School, he went to California in search of something better. According to his own later recollections, he held a number of nondescript jobs while there. According to the evidence unearthed by his most recent biographer, he actually spent most of his time in California working in the law office of his cousin. Stymied by his lack of the necessary training and credentials, Johnson returned to Texas in 1926 at age 17, where, among other jobs, he worked as a pick and shovel man and operated a "fresno" drawn by four mules, in a road building project run by the state highway department. Before entering college two years later, he taught for a short time in a Mexican school in south Texas.

At San Marcos Teachers College, which he later described as inexpensive, familiar, and close to home, Johnson was compelled to take on a number of jobs, working as a member of a cleanup crew, janitor, and, most advantageously, as a special assistant to the school president. Johnson was an indifferent student, since learning for the sake of learning seems to have bored him. But he proved himself brilliantly adept at manipulating both the school administration and the student body, doing so silently and subtly. He attained a kind of make-or-break power over young men and women desperate for the jobs that he had the power to dispense. On graduating from San Marcos, Johnson taught school, first in the small town of Pearsall and then in Houston, where he scored a dazzling success during his short tenure as teacher of public speaking. But his heart and his greatest skills were in politics, as he demonstrated by the masterful campaign he organized for Willy Hopkins in Hopkins's successful race for the Texas state senate. Johnson's efforts earned him a rich dividend, for it was primarily because of Hopkins's recommendation that the newly elected Texas congressman Richard Kleberg in 1931 chose to take the twenty-two-year-old Johnson with him to Washington as his secretary and chief assistant. The position turned out to be a turning point in Johnson's career.

It was not simply that he held the job for four years. Since Kleberg cannot unfairly be described as a playboy millionaire (part owner of the fabulous King Ranch, an empire that in size dwarfed many of the nation's states), it was Johnson who did the myriad jobs that went with congressional office. In the process he learned and honed the political skills that were later to earn him recognition as "super Lyndon," and he did his work ostentatiously enough to leave no doubts in the minds of the mighty that it was he who did it.

During his tenure with Kleberg, Johnson met and on the night of their meeting proposed to Claudia (Lady Bird) Taylor, who shortly surrendered to his fervent importuning. He married up, since Miss Taylor, like the two young women he had earlier courted, was the daughter of the richest man in town. Her family were more genteel, prestigious, and wealthy than his own. Her father Thomas Taylor was a businessman and landowner in Karnack, Texas. His wife was the daughter of a rich planter who owned the largest estate in his home community of Evergreen, Alabama. Lady Bird Taylor was a graduate of the University of Texas in Austin, an institution not far geographically from San Marcos but light-years beyond it in prestige. Although this shy young woman was rich enough to have no need to work and had an "open charge account" at the exclusive Nieman-Marcus store in Dallas, she was enrolled in a graduate school of journalism when she met Johnson. It was her inheritance money that the couple used to buy a small radio station from which they subsequently earned millions.

A year after the marriage, Johnson, who had ingratiated himself with the mighty Sam Rayburn, was named director of the National Youth Administration for Texas. Opportunity again knocked the following year, 1937, and Johnson was again ready, this time winning the special election for congressman from Texas, made necessary by the sudden death of the incumbent from a nearby congressional district. Johnson's victory was made possible in part by the $10,000 "lent" him by his father-in-law and by the untold additional thousands given his campaign by oil companies and friendly businessmen. Great public friend to the New Deal—his campaign slogan and his essential tactic in the Congressional contest was to cry, "Roosevelt and Supreme Court Reorganization!"— Johnson received the lavish moneys he did because he was the great secret friend to powerful business interests, particularly the mighty magnate Charles Marsh and above all the brothers Herman and George Brown. It was largely through Congressman Johnson's extraordinary behind-the-scenes labors in behalf of their firm, Brown and Root, that they were awarded noncompetitive government contracts to build dams and naval bases that earned them hundreds of millions of dollars in profit. The Browns never forgot such favors and handsomely rewarded the politician responsible for them—so handsomely, in fact, that their violations of the Corrupt Practices Act, in funneling, illegally, hundreds of thousands of dollars to Johnson's campaign to win a seat in the U.S. Senate in the special election of 1941, would have put an ignominious end to Johnson's political career but for the providential decision by the national administration to call off an investigation that seemed likely to result in criminal charges.

The Roosevelt administration's support of LBJ's senatorial race in 1941 was reward for the brilliant job he had done in revitalizing the moribund Democratic Congressional Campaign Committee during the presidential election of 1940. And FDR loved Johnson for the support he had given the plan to dump John Nance Garner of Texas from the national ticket in 1940. Thereafter all government contracts for Texas required Johnson's approval. The reason Johnson did not run in the regular senatorial election in 1942 is that he had promised, while campaigning for the special seat the previous year, that he would join his fellow Texans "in the trenches" if war broke out. After Pearl Harbor he served, not in the trenches but in the navy as a lieutenant commander for part of one year. Evidently blessed with a faulty memory, Johnson later spoke of having flown on many missions. In fact, while visiting General MacArthur's headquarters for FDR, Johnson chose to accompany a crew on *one* bombing mission. To the dismay of the men who did the shooting and navigating during that flight, it was Johnson alone who was rewarded with what one writer has called, "one of the least deserved but most often displayed Silver Stars in American military history." (That judgment may be unfair; in World War II this writer witnessed the awarding of even more prestigious medals to officers for having done nothing more than observe from a distance the fighting being done by front-line infantrymen.) When FDR issued a directive on July 19, 1942, urging congressmen in the military service to "return to inactive duty, except those who wished to stay in uniform," Johnson was one of the few congressmen who elected to return immediately to Congress.

After his election to the U.S. Senate in 1948, Johnson enjoyed meteoric success. Midway through his first term he became majority whip, two years later minority leader, and almost immediately after his reelection in 1954 he was designated majority leader. Although, in the words of a sympathetic biographer, "Johnson kept the doors to his financial history tightly closed," it is clear that he had become a rich man by the time he won the Democratic vice-presidential nomination in 1960. It is equally clear that his wealth owed little to mere senatorial income. His very rich friend Charles Marsh sold him valuable real estate for a small fraction of its value. The brothers Brown did numerous services that enhanced the value of his property and they did them gratis. And the bankrupt Austin radio station KTBC that the Johnsons had bought for $17,500 in 1943 was within ten years worth more than a hundred times that amount and shortly afterwards netting more than half a million dollars a year. As Johnson's confidante carefully observes, the station was helped by a "long string of favorable decisions handed down by the F.C.C. [with Johnson himself] inevitably involved in all the major decisions concerning the status and personnel of the F.C.C." Johnson invested his radio profits in land and bank securities. Shortly after he became president, he told a press conference that he owned "a little ranch, something in excess of 2,000 acres." The disclosure was disingenuous, for it said nothing of the thousands of acres he owned and controlled under the names of other men. *Life* magazine estimated that Johnson was worth $14 million when he entered the White House.

Disappointed at having to settle for the second spot on the national ticket, Johnson three years later became the fourth vice-president to reach the highest office because of the assassination of a president.

Richard M. Nixon was the first president who owed his political rise above all to an anticommunist ideology or, to put it perhaps more precisely, to a public career guided above all by militant anticommunism. Whatever the ultimate source of Nixon's political ideas may have been, certainly they owed nothing to the great wealth and genteel upbringing that explains the philosophical conservatism of some men. During the president's youth, the Nixons lived modestly at best on the profits earned by the small family store. When unanticipated disaster struck, in the form of the tuberculosis contracted by Nixon's older brother, the family was almost ruined financially by the expense of sending Harold Nixon to Tucson, where he had to be looked after by his mother, and by the financial drain resulting from the maintenance of two households. Frank Nixon had to sell half the land on which his store stood in order to meet his bills; the president's recollection is that the family subsisted largely on canned foods and candy bars for breakfasts, while he himself had to wear hand-me-downs. Before he was sent off at seventeen to Whittier College, Nixon worked hard in his father's store, putting in a working day that often began at three or four in the morning and involved driving a truck to market for vegetables, pumping gas, delivering groceries, and setting up displays. After he entered college he took over as manager of the vegetable department and bookkeeper of the store, and supplemented his income by working as a handyman and janitor for a public swimming pool, among other jobs. After graduating from college, Nixon won a full-tuition scholarship to Duke University Law School. Even while he was a law student, Nixon took a job with the National Youth Administration, earning 35 cents an hour.

Not getting a tumble either from the FBI or the big law firms to which he applied after completing his courses at Duke, Nixon at age 24 returned home to practice law with Whittier's oldest legal firm but a firm that was nevertheless very small. Within two years he became "town attorney" in La Habia, a lawyerless nearby community with a population of four thousand, and an attorney, prosecutor in police court, and "sort of overseer of law enforcement" in Whittier. His attempts to dabble in business on the side did not pay off. In 1940 he married Thelma Ryan, a young woman of family no more successful or eminent than Nixon's. An orphan at thirteen, "Pat" Ryan as a young girl had worked in a hospital in the Bronx before returning to California, where her parents had lived, to attend the University of Southern California. Though she graduated with honors, the jobs she subsequently got were as waitress and salesgirl. And she did not make it in Hollywood. When Nixon married her, she was teaching commercial subjects in Whittier High School.

After Pearl Harbor, Nixon worked for a short time in Washington, D.C., in the office of price administration. In summer, 1942, he joined the navy as lieutenant junior grade. Although he was eventually promoted to lieutenant commander and spent more than a year in the Pacific theatre, Nixon's naval career was undramatic and not particularly distinguished. One of the highlights of his war experience was his success as a poker player. Nixon won more than $10,000 and after the war proceeded to put this money to effective political use. In 1946 he put aside half his winnings to finance his campaign for congressman from the 26th congressional district in California. Nixon got the job as Republican candidate by responding to the ad the party had placed in more than two dozen newspapers: "Wanted: congressional candidate with no previous political experience. . . . Any young man resident of this district, preferably a veteran [with] fair education may apply for the job." In what was to become a famous—or infamous—campaign, Nixon defeated Jerry Voorhis, the longtime Democratic incumbent, with the aid of ads stating: "A vote for Nixon is a vote against the Communist-dominated PAC with its gigantic slush fund." The rest, as they say, is history.

Riding the wave of postwar anticommunism, Nixon was reelected in 1948 and in 1950 he easily won the contest for the U.S. Senate against the Democratic candidate, Helen Gahagan Douglas, labeled by Nixon as the "pink lady." Exploiting the red issue more astutely than had any other politician, including the soon to be destroyed Senator Joe McCarthy, Nixon was in 1952 elected vice-president, only six years after emerging from the deepest obscurity. In 1960 he lost by a whisker to John F. Kennedy in the presidential contest. When two years later he was defeated in his bid for the California governorship, some people thought that his career was over and that, in his words, the press "wouldn't have Dick Nixon to kick around anymore." They were wrong of course. In 1968 Nixon won a close contest with Hubert Humphrey and in 1972 an overwhelming victory over George McGovern.

During the 1960s Nixon had no trouble becoming a quite rich man. His extremely wealthy supporter, Elmer Bobst, chairman of the board at Warner-Lambert Pharmaceutical, secured Nixon a senior partnership in the large New York City law firm of Mudge, Rose, Guthrie, and Alexander, which handled Bobst's business. Solicitor now for some of the largest corporations in the world, neighbor of Nelson D. Rockefeller and occupant of an expensive and lavish New York City apartment, hugely successful investor in undervalued real estate, sought-after lecturer and writer, member of New York City's most fashionable and prestigious clubs, intimate of its richest and most powerful men as they dined at 21 and the Waldorf, the former vice-president was a great worldly success, a tribute to the great opportunities open to opportunistic men possessed of the necessary acumen. Late in his vice-presidential tenure, Nixon told Earl Mazo that he owned no real estate and his "net worth [was] pretty small." A decade later, on the eve of his ascension to the presidency, Nixon moved in business and social circles inhabited solely by multimillionaires and enjoyed a life-style closely akin to theirs.

The most striking feature of Gerald Ford's youth is that it was not until he was seventeen that he learned that Leslie King was his father, that he himself had been born Leslie Lynch King, and that Gerald R. Ford, his mother's second husband, was his stepfather. Raised in upper-middle-class comfort as a youngster, Ford did various odd jobs in his stepfather's paint factory. When, as a high school senior in 1930, he took a part-time job washing dishes and waiting on tables at a local restaurant, he did so not so much to keep busy as to help out a family that, like most others of the time, was hurt by the onset of the Great Depression. A star lineman at Grand Rapids High School, Ford won a football scholarship to the University of Michigan. After graduating in 1935, Ford was hired as assistant football coach and boxing coach at Yale at a salary of $2400 per year, a job he held for almost six years. During this period, Ford invested $1,000 in the Conover model agency and was himself a model for a short time. He also entered Yale University Law School in 1938, at first as a part-time student, earning his law degree three years later. He returned to Grand Rapids where he and a friend started a law firm that during its brief year of existence had only a "meager practice." In spring, 1942, Ford joined the navy, entering as an ensign. By the time he was discharged three and a half years later, he had risen to the rank of lieutenant commander.

After the war, Ford joined a stable law firm at a salary of

$3600 per year. He also showed an interest in the politics of Kent County, Michigan, where his stepfather had become Republican county chairman. In 1948 Ford ran for Congress and, during the campaign, wooed Mrs. Betty Bloomer Warren, the daughter of a manufacturer's representative, whom he married a few weeks before the election. Mrs. Warren, who had divorced her first husband, was a fashion coordinator at a department store who had earlier attended Bennington College and studied dance with Martha Graham. Ford's victory in this campaign was abetted by the fact that he kept his marriage a secret in a congressional district known to harbor a significant number of voters opposed to divorce. Ford spent the following twenty-four years in Congress, serving as minority leader of the House during the last eight years of his tenure. In December, 1973, in the wake of the disgrace of Spiro T. Agnew, Ford became the first man ever to be appointed vice-president. The following year, after the disgrace and resignation of Richard M. Nixon, the man who had appointed him vice-president, Ford became the first man ever to become president of the United States during the administration of an incumbent who was still alive.

James Earl Carter, Jr., grew up just outside of Plains, Georgia, where his father operated a farm and general store. If, as Carter recalled, the family's farm work "was heavy all year round," it was because they were kept busy by the elder Carter's "widely diversified farm industries." According to the future president's mother, the family had a "nice house," "always had a car," and had "the first radio in Plains." Their level of living is suggested too by the fact that in common with everyone else in the community during Jimmy Carter's boyhood they relied on an outdoor privy and a hand pump for water, and had neither electricity nor running water in their house. Although Carter grew up during the Depression, his family experienced no economic hardship and always had plenty to eat. The strenuous but enjoyable work the young farm boy did was occasioned not by hard times but, as he later observed, by the very scope and success of the family's enterprises. As a boy of five, Carter was making a dollar a day selling boiled peanuts on the streets of Plains, sometimes making five times that sum on Saturdays. Remarkably, he was able to earn enough from these entrepreneurial activities to be able, after age 9, to speculate modestly but profitably in bales of cotton and to buy homes from which he said he collected $16.50 a month in rents. He evidently owned these houses for about fifteen years before selling them in 1949 while he was a naval officer in Hawaii. Dreaming almost from infancy of a military career, Carter was in 1943 accepted in the U.S. Naval Academy at Annapolis, after spending the previous year as a naval R.O.T.C. student at Georgia Tech. In his autobiography, Carter observes that receiving an "assured" education at a public institution was "no small consideration" during what he erroneously calls "those early depression years." Actually, he had first attended Georgia Southwestern Junior College after graduating from high school, and his decision to go to Annapolis seems to have had more to do with his father's enthusiastic support for such an education and his own youthful dreams than with financial stringency.

Shortly after being commissioned an ensign on graduating from the Naval Academy in 1946, Carter married Rosalynn Smith, a young family friend. Miss Smith's father was said to be an "indirect descendant" of the famous Captain John Smith. During his daughter's youth, however, he worked as a mechanic and as the bus driver for the Plains school. After her father's death when Rosalynn was thirteen, her mother took in sewing and worked in a grocery, before becoming the head of the Plains post office. She saved sufficient money to be able to send Miss Smith to the Georgia Southwestern College in Americus that Carter himself had earlier attended. Carter spent seven years as an officer in the navy, much of it as a specially trained submarine officer. On his father's death late in 1953, Carter, now twenty-nine, decided to resign from the navy and take over the family business.

Fortified by the several thousand dollars he had saved in the navy and by his inheritance, Carter survived a difficult first year to go on to substantial success as a businessman farmer. Within fifteen years the Carters were earning a gross income of almost one million dollars a year, most of it from the Carter warehouse, the rest from a variety of activities including several partnerships and real estate in neighboring counties. Clearly an ambitious man, Carter found time in the 1950s to become active in many organizations. He reports that he was state president of the certified seed organization, district governor of Lions International, chairman of the local planning commission, president of the Georgia planning association, a member of the library board and hospital authority, and first a member and later chairman of the Sumter County school board. After he became a leading figure in politics he was named chairman of the March of Dimes. In the fall of 1962 he was elected to the first of two terms in the Georgia state senate. After losing in the Democratic primary contest for governor in 1966, Carter worked indefatigably to secure the nomination in 1970 and easily won the fall election. Prevented by law from a second term, Carter cast his eye on a still loftier executive position. After being named chairman of the national Democratic campaign committee in 1974, Carter two years later charmed the party into naming him its candidate for president.

Most of what has been written of Ronald Reagan's youth is based on his own recollections. At fourteen, while a student in high school, he had a summer job with a construction contractor. The next year and for six summers following, he worked as lifeguard at a riverfront recreation area near Dixon, Illinois. In this job he says he saved seventy-seven people from drowning. When he enrolled in Eureka College, a small Disciples of Christ college near Peoria, Reagan was assisted by the $400 he had saved from his summer jobs and by a half-tuition athletic scholarship. At college he washed dishes for a fraternity house, taught swimming, and worked in the kitchen of the girls' dormitory. An indifferent student, in part because at Dixon High School he had "never bothered to do much more than remain eligible for the athletic teams," Reagan continued at college to care more about making the football team than about learning. He made the football team only after languishing on the bench during his freshman year and beginning his second season with the fifth team. (His memory may be faulty here, for it is doubtful that Eureka's small squad numbered even thirty players.) He explains that he was moved up to the second team after a scrimmage in which a friend tipped him off in advance of each offensive play run by Reagan's opponents, allowing him to look like a better player than in fact he was. (As I write, the question has been raised whether Reagan knew that he had been tipped off in advance about what President Carter would say in their televised debate in 1980.) He evidently read very little in college but as he was later to say, "there is more to college than books."

After graduating in 1932, Reagan returned home for one more summer as a lifeguard but he soon landed a job announcing University of Iowa football games for radio station WOC in Davenport. He was paid five dollars plus fare for his first game and ten dollars for subsequent games. Early in 1934 he was made a staff announcer and was shortly making $75 a week announcing football, baseball, track, and swimming for WHO in Des Moines, Iowa, the "key station" for NBC in the midwest. He had enough imagination to announce Cubs and White Sox games without seeing them, embellishing laconic Western Union reports with detailed inventions of what Billy Herman, Gabby Hartnett, Ted Lyons, and the other players were supposedly doing on the diamond. In 1937, while covering the Cubs spring training camp in Catalina, Reagan auditioned for Warner Brothers. He quickly accepted their offer of a contract at $200 a week. At first confined to B films and occasional bit parts in A films, Reagan soon scored in his roles as George Gipp (to Pat O'Brian's Knute Rockne) and General Custer (to Errol Flynn's Jeb Stuart). Within five years he was earning $3,500 a week on his new seven-year contract. In 1940 he married the film star Jane Wyman. The marriage foundered after her career surpassed his; she sued for divorce in 1948. Reagan four years later married Nancy Davis, a little-known film actress. She was the daughter of Kenneth Robbins and Edith Luckett Robbins. Robbins has been described as a man of means, descended from "an old New England family with a big house, money in . . . woolen mills, and proud traditions." Nancy's mother was an obscure actress, whose taste for the theater was born when, as a child, she visited the theater her uncle managed in Richmond, Virginia. Since Nancy's parents were estranged, and her mother grew unhappy with the routine of carrying the infant from theater engagement to theater engagement, "using trunks as cradles," Edith brought the child at age 2 to live with her married older sister in Bethesda, Maryland. Nancy had a comfortable middle-class upbringing. Just before her eighth birthday, her mother married Dr. Loyal Davis, a successful and wealthy surgeon. At fourteen Nancy chose to be formally adopted by her stepfather, her name then becoming Nancy Davis. Miss Davis attended exclusive private schools in Chicago and Smith College in Northampton, Massachusetts. According to some critics, her admired social standing opened doors for her in Hollywood that might otherwise have remained closed to a young woman of modest talents.

Ronald Reagan is today an accomplished actor. Several critics think, however, that whatever early success he enjoyed in Hollywood owed more to his physical appearance and the friendships he cultivated with producers and columnists like Hedda Hopper and Louella Parsons than to acting ability. Reagan was a somewhat wooden figure on the screen, and there is some question whether he was the star he evidently thinks he was. Yet he did achieve national recognition and he was a success in dollar terms, if a modest success by true star standards. "The Errol Flynn of the B's," according to Reagan's self-appraisal of his early Hollywood years, he neither played the lead nor scored an outstanding success when he did appear in major films. After World War II he was relegated mainly to cowboy pictures; by the late forties his "career was petering out in one humiliation after another," as he played in a series of second-rate films.

The second world war turned out to be a pleasant interlude in Reagan's career. According to Laurence Leamer, after Reagan was accepted by the U.S. Cavalry as a second lieutenant, he was "ticketed for 'limited service'" because of his near-sightedness. Leamer reports that Reagan "smilingly would have marched out of the theater into the hell throes of battle." Instead, Reagan spent the war not in battle but in Hollywood as a personnel officer in the army air force, narrating and occasionally acting in training films. Unlike Sterling Hayden and James Stewart, actors who engaged in combat overseas, and unlike that great number of men who fought in the front-line infantry despite ailments worse than his, Reagan passed the war under attractive conditions that, according to Laurence Leamer, "most Americans would not have dreamed possible for themselves." By the early 1950s, when his film career appeared to be slowing down, Reagan became an "unofficial spokesman" of the film industry. In 1954 he landed an attractive job first at $125,000 per year and soon after at $150,000 with the General Electric Corporation. For the next eight years he was the emcee for its new television series and a super salesman of the company's products; he also visited GE plants to try to improve workers' morale. When the TV series suffered a viewer slump, in 1962, Reagan's job ended. Unemployment was brief and painless while it did last, since Reagan was by now a rich man with large real estate holdings. With the help of his brother, who was vice-president of a large advertising agency, Reagan was hired in 1964 by the U.S. Borax corporation to host the series, "Death Valley Days." By 1966 he was the Republican party's nominee for governor of California, ousting Pat Brown, the Democratic incumbent, in the fall election.

Like Richard Nixon, Ronald Reagan owed much of his political currency to his widely known and militant anticommunism. By his own admission, Reagan had been a liberal early in his Hollywood career and ostensibly "bled for 'causes.'" True, he had been an early member of the Screen Actors Guild and for several years its president. Yet in 1947, when Hollywood liberals were attacking the House Un-American Activities Committee, Reagan supported its activities and appeared as a friendly witness before it, urging that unfriendly witnesses be blacklisted. He may, as he says he did, have voted for Democratic presidential candidates until 1952 and switched to the Republican party only a decade later. Yet as GE spokesman he had denounced public medical care for the aged, urban renewal, TVA, and welfare legislation, and had said that the graduated income tax was "spawned by Karl Marx" and "the prime essential of a socialist state." He no doubt meant these things he said. In the early 1960s he did yeoman service for conservative Republicanism, eliciting from Barry Goldwater a declaration that he would "gladly serve with, under, or alongside" Ronald Reagan. To prepare for his gubernatorial campaign in 1966, he hired the services of the Spence-Robert agency, which tutored him in the ways of separating corporate officers from large contributions of money and in convincing the electorate of his humanity and even his erudition. Actually, he needed little advice on how to please monied men for he had been pleasing them at least since his days as GE spokesman. He was reelected governor of California in 1970 but chose not to seek a third term in 1974, having set his sights higher. After narrowly losing the primary battle for the Republican presidential nomination in 1976 to Gerald Ford, Reagan four years later succeeded first in becoming his party's choice and then the nation's for president of the United States.

These prepresidential careers recount an almost unbroken catalogue of success stories. In a society which ranks law as one of the most prestigious occupations and typically places a fraction of one percent of adult males in the profession, more than two-thirds of the presidents were lawyers or trained for the law. And as the careers of most of the lawyer-presidents make clear, they were unusually successful attorneys with lucrative practices, who had had the good fortune to read or train with wealthy and eminent masters or to attend prestigious law schools. Their careers in the law contrasted sharply with the legal careers of most of the nation's lawyers. The presidents were indeed the crème de la crème of the legal profession—at least when judged by a worldly standard.

It is of course not surprising that more than two-thirds of the presidents had been earlier active and successful in politics, with more than fifty percent in the House of Representatives, almost forty percent in the Senate, and close to fifty percent state governors. The fact remains that—in all understatement—these were positions of great prestige and high salaries, certainly when compared with the jobs done and the income earned by the great mass of Americans in the lower and the lower middle classes. In these respects, the presidents were if anything even less similar to the American people than were their parents and grandparents.

A well-known political scientist has written that "the president of the United States is not really required to be a college graduate." And yet, in contrast to the less than three percent of the eligible population attending college before 1900, seventy percent of the presidents attended. Certainly there is no constitutional provision requiring presidents to have a higher education. It is simply good sense that the nation's chief executive officer be well educated. (Alas, their mere attendance at college does not assure that they will be.) The only point I am here making is that in their education, as in most other measurable respects, the presidents have been most unlike the American people.

Nor do the brief social portraits I have drawn express all of the significant dissimilarities between our leaders and the people they have led. In their religious affiliations, for example, the presidents appear to have been almost as much unlike their constituents as they were in their occupations and education. I speak of affiliations rather than convictions or beliefs not only because the latter two terms are harder to pin down or measure but also because religious affiliation is probably a better clue than are religious beliefs to a person's social standing. Since there are rich Catholics, Methodists, and Baptists as well as poor ones, socially low Episcopalians, Presbyterians, and Congregationalists as well as eminent ones, and similar splits among all the other sects, faiths, and denominations, religious affiliation or church membership is not an infallible clue to an individual's social standing. But there is a great deal of evidence correlating socially dissimilar *groups* of people to some churches and religions rather than to others. The interesting fact is that most of the presidents appear to have been affiliated with Protestant denominations that, when combined, have contained less than ten and at times less than five percent of the American population. That is, the presidents were connected inordinately with the high-prestige denominations—the Episcopalians, the Presbyterians, the Unitarians, the Dutch Reformed Church, the Quakers—all of which contain unusually high proportions or percentages of professionals and businessmen in their memberships. Very few presidents have been Baptists, Methodists, or Catholics—the churches that have usually enrolled most of the nation's Christian population.

I speak with less than certitude of the presidents' religious affiliations because that is all that the evidence properly permits. Those popular summaries of presidential characteristics that with no ifs or buts list "the presidents' religious affiliations and beliefs" speak with an assurance that is not warranted by the evidence. For in the case of a fair number of the presidents, they never made it clear which, if any, denomination they preferred. That is why different authorities on the presidents' religion offer different estimates or "box scores" of their affiliations and memberships. For an example of some of the problems attending this matter, Polk, who on his mother's side was a descendant of John Knox, the Scottish founder of Presbyterianism, was a "financial pillar" of the Presbyterian church, whose services he and Mrs. Polk usually attended. Yet when Mrs. Polk for some reason could not go to church, Polk would attend the Methodist church. As he got older, Polk spoke of joining the church and though his mother brought a Presbyterian minister to baptize him, he finally turned to Methodism. Other presidents too changed their preferences and it is not always clear precisely when. Pierce, nominally a Congregationalist, attended Presbyterian and Episcopalian churches. Cleveland belonged to no church but attended Presbyterian services, while Theodore Roosevelt we are told had both Presbyterian and Dutch Reformed "leanings."

Since most of the presidents began from an unusually high starting point, it was indeed hard if not impossible for them to climb dramatically. How much higher than their loftily situated parents and grandparents could Washington, Jefferson, Madison, Monroe, John Quincy Adams, the Harrisons, Tyler, Polk, Taylor, Taft, the two Roosevelts, Wilson, and Kennedy possibly go? Yet those who commenced life from a social level beneath the lightly populated upper classes almost without exception did indeed rise. Particularly dramatic examples were Jackson, Fillmore, Lincoln, Andrew Johnson, Garfield, Hoover, Eisenhower, Nixon, and Reagan. Perhaps Grant came closest as an adult to failure, never approximating before the Civil War the material success of his father. But the war did come and he responded so remarkably that in its aftermath lavish material gifts were showered on him.

The great question is: What accounted for the presidents' success before they reached the White House? The answer differs for each president and is of course compounded of many parts, none of them susceptible to precise measurement. In the chapter that follows, I shall examine the part that their family standing and early advantages seem to have played in propelling them toward the presidency. In so doing, I shall have to consider too the part played by their own "merits" and their own performance. Inevitably, questions will remain about the causes of their achievement.

What is not in question is that without exception the men selected for the presidency were men who achieved great worldly success not dreamed of by the "average citizen" of the United States.

☆☆☆☆☆ CHAPTER FIVE ☆☆☆☆☆

The Influence of the Presidents' Origins on Their Adult Success

ALMOST ALL THE PRESIDENTS achieved great worldly success before ascending to the highest office. The question is, to what extent was this success due to the privileged birth and upbringing most of them enjoyed?

While it is a question that no serious discussion of this theme can avoid addressing, it is a question that can not be answered definitively. Ascertaining the causes of any individual's success is a difficult and sensitive task. It is impossible to isolate and affix a precise significance to the relative part played by native mental and physical endowment, character, ambition, drive, or luck, and the part played by family advantages in wealth, standing, prestige, and influence in accounting for any one's success. Success, like failure or any other destination, is explained not by any single cause but by a combination of causes. In life these causes are of course intertwined with one another. Disentangling them and trying to isolate one from all the others in order to try to estimate its role is an artificial exercise. And yet it is a valuable exercise. That it can not be performed perfectly does not mean that it can not be performed usefully. To be performed usefully, it must be based on a substantial amount of appropriate evidence that is sensibly interpreted. A sensible interpretation of the influence of a man's early circumstances on his career requires an understanding of the possible limits of this influence.

It is, for example, widely believed that if someone born to wealth and high social position subsequently enjoys great success in life, his later good fortune is due primarily if not entirely to his advantages at birth. But this is not necessarily so. It is conceivable that he might have risen high even in the absence of his youthful advantages. The only proper way to deal with the question is to make no assumptions about the supposed dominant influence of a man's early circumstances on his adult career, but rather patiently to sift through as much evidence as possible for signs of what seemed to account for whatever success he achieved in life. Fortunately, there is a good deal of useful evidence on the lives of the presidents.

Several of the presidents do appear to have been self-made men, whose success owed little or nothing to their circumstances at birth and almost everything to their own exertions. The most striking feature of this rags-to-riches pattern was its uncommonness; only Fillmore, Andrew Johnson, and, to a lesser extent, Lincoln, qualify. Lincoln's father and his ancestors on the paternal side were, as we have seen, more secure economically and more highly placed socially than popular legend has it. And yet, Lincoln's decision to become a lawyer and the stature he quickly achieved in the profession, like his decision to enter politics, appear to have been abetted not at all by family wealth or prominence. The problematic prominence of Johnson's father or, to put it more precisely, his surprisingly friendly relations with some of his community's leading men, did not enable his son to escape a youth of poverty and want after the elder Johnson drowned. Nor did it prevent him from being apprenticed at fourteen. Like Johnson, Fillmore too was apprenticed at fourteen. When at nineteen he began to read for the law and four years later to practice the profession, he appears in both instances to have depended almost entirely on his own ambition and efforts. A political career opened up for him as a result of the wealth and prominence his own performance as an attorney earned for him. While a devil's advocate might argue that Fillmore's unusual good fortune in first reading for the law with a well-known and wealthy lawyer may have owed something to his family's good name, just as Lincoln's election to the state legislature may also have been abetted, no matter how slightly, by his father's modest standing, I think it more reasonable to adjudge both presidents as examples of men who achieved success as adults through their own efforts alone.

Only a fine line separates Fillmore, Lincoln, and Andrew Johnson from Garfield, Nixon, and Reagan. Garfield's father was far from rich, but as the future president's mother rightly insisted, neither was the family poor. As a boy, young Garfield was sent to a private academy, then to a private institute, and finally to an excellent college, institutions all far beyond the range of most Americans at mid-nineteenth century. Nor was he a great intellect. As his sympathetic mentor at college conceded, Garfield was without "pretence of genius." As men who rose to the top of the political heap above all by their exploitation of the nation's fear of communism, Nixon and Reagan and the careers they carved out may not command universal admiration. The fact remains that their success, no matter how controversial, appears to have owed far more to their own performance as adults than it does to the modest advantages their families conferred on them. Yet Nixon at seventeen was able to attend college at a time when few Americans of college age could dream of doing so. Reagan's college education may have been financed almost entirely by his own modest savings from his summer jobs and a half-tuition athletic scholarship; nevertheless, he was a member of that select minority of young Americans whose families could spare them from the necessity of earning income during their late teen years. I am not saying that family support was a crucial element in the rise of Richard Nixon or Ronald Reagan. In the balance of factors that explain the rise of any man, the greatest weight by far must be assigned the shrewdness and the opportunism of the one, the personality, charm, and glibness of the other. Yet they did receive a slight but not totally insignificant boost from their families at the outset of their careers as young adults. Could Nixon have answered that ad for a Republican congressional candidate were he not a "college man"? Would Reagan have been at Catalina with the Chicago Cubs had he not put in the time he did at college?

The balance shifts slightly in the direction of greater family influence on the careers of Truman and Eisenhower. Harry Truman's difficulties as a small businessman after World War I have blinded many of us to the fact that as a young man in his twenties and early thirties, he ran the unusually substantial and profitable farm his family had inherited from his mother's parents. He was later able to make the fairly large investment he did in a haberdashery because of the money he had made from his inheritance. And it was because of his family's standing as well as his service record that Truman was sounded out by his local Democratic party for a judgeship shortly after the war ended. Eisenhower's father, while no smashing success as a businessman, did manage to earn a far better income than most skilled artisans in the dairy firm of his sister's husband—the same plant in which young Eisenhower worked as a foreman after high school. And the family was able to afford having Ike attend West Point.

Presidents Jackson, Van Buren, Grant, Hoover, and Lyndon Johnson were men of outstanding ability, each of them achieving striking success before rising to the presidency and each clearly owing that success above all to his own capacity, acumen, and performance. Yet each of them did have a significant head start in the race. They capitalized on their advantages, true, but these were rare advantages nevertheless and helped catapult them forward in "life's competition."

The way was paved for Jackson's early entry into the Tennessee "aristocracy" as young lawyer, property owner, speculator, soldier, and man of action by his reading for the law, while yet a teenager, with men of unusual influence and standing. He could do so because his inheritance and the standing of his mother's relatives had placed him in the higher echelons of backcountry Tennessee society. It was of course his unique blending of character and fighting ability—whether against personal enemies, Indian tribes, or English troops—that captured the attention of contemporaries. One suspects that Jackson would have risen high no matter what the milieu he started from. The fact is, however, that he spent his youthful years on a social level that was comparatively lofty; living on this level opened up opportunities that otherwise would have been closed off to him. He did take full advantage of these opportunities. Yet there is reason to wonder whether a youngster similarly courageous, ambitious, strong, and single-minded as Jackson, but a youngster receiving no inheritance and brought up in a humble family surrounded by poverty, could have achieved as much as Jackson. To doubt the possibility that such a youth might fail despite these attributes is to assume the validity of that ancient chestnut, comforting to the haves of the earth, that those who fail to make it fail because of their personal deficiencies. To put it most gently, this thesis is unproven.

Martin Van Buren showed himself to be a man of great ability and shrewdness well before he aspired to the White House. Rightly regarded in his own time as the most masterful of politicians, he had also demonstrated uncommon capacity as a lawyer, accumulating a sizeable fortune as he simultaneously built his two careers. There can, however, be no denying that his success was significantly aided by youthful opportunities available to few contemporaries, first to attend a private academy and then to read for the law with a man of great distinction and wide contacts. The respect commanded by his family and perhaps by the high standing of his mother's first husband were no doubt helpful in securing the latter opportunity.

In the phrase of his most recent biographer, Grant had "no organic, artistic, or intellectual specialness." Grant of course made himself an invincible presidential candidate by his own prowess as general in the Union army. He became an officer by having a relatively privileged private school education and attending West Point—opportunities, both, that owed something to the uncommon business success enjoyed by his father. Herbert Hoover achieved a success in engineering and business that was comparable, if not as dramatic or as newsworthy, to Grant's and, like Grant, he did so by his own efforts. Like Grant, too, Hoover got an important boost as a youth, in Hoover's case from the influential uncle who provided him a superior education. Lyndon Johnson ably exploited his early involvements, first with a Texas state senator and then with a member of Congress, to make his own mark in politics. For all his poor-mouthing of his youth, Johnson was the son of a man who himself had had a noted career in Texas politics; the younger Johnson was able to attend college and after college do white collar work, and he found the doors to a political career opening to him in Texas largely because important men thought well of his father.

Although Gerald Ford's stepfather was a relatively successful upper-middle-class businessman, Ford was able to attend the University of Michigan because of the athletic scholarship he won by his own prowess as a football player. And his record as a college football star earned him the coaching jobs at Yale that enabled him subsequently to enroll at Yale Law School. As a man who spent most of his adult years as a member of the House of Representatives from Michigan, Ford owed his start in county politics largely to his stepfather's leadership of the Republican party in Kent County, Michigan.

It is not to detract from their ability to note that most of the others, or close to two-thirds of all the presidents, owed much of their adult success to youthful advantages that were great enough to enable them easily, almost effortlessly, to attain unusually lofty station. Lucrative private careers and prestigious political offices beckoned not because these presidents had shown themselves to be young men of special quality but because they were born into families of special distinction, great wealth, or admired standing. The point is not that they were lacking in "special quality" but only that it does not appear to have been a factor in getting them started in what was clearly the right direction.

The sheer intellectual brilliance early demonstrated by John Adams, Jefferson, Madison, John Quincy Adams, Taft, and Wilson suggests that each might have risen to great heights even without his advantages of birth. But there is of course no way of separating out their privileged youthful positions from the other elements, including innate capacity, that went into their success.

Child to the second most prestigious and influential family in Braintree, Massachusetts, John Adams naturally attended Harvard and when he prepared for a career in the law, did so under the tutelage of the leading lawyer in Boston. Adams might have stumbled despite this advantageous beginning, had he lacked the necessary traits of mind and character. The fact remains that the inside track that was open to Adams both in professional and public life appears to have rested more on the distinction of his family than on prepossessing characteristics that, as a matter of fact, as a young man he had hardly had an opportunity to exhibit.

As Jefferson's most distinguished biographer observed, the "most important fact" of his early career was his "assured family position." Born to a wealthy and aristocratic Virginia family, the youthful Jefferson was educated by private tutors, attended William and Mary College, read for the law with a great eminence, and on beginning his practice was sought after by the richest and most influential clients. He seemed simply to step into the privileged station and influential positions in religious, social, and political life that in his time were monopolized by men of great family. His magnificent breadth of intellectual, scientific, and artistic interests, not to mention his marvelous range of abilities, would subsequently charm generations of scholars, as they charmed and impressed many of his contemporaries. Yet, it takes nothing away from his own capacity to observe that the expensive travel and education which allowed him to satisfy his vast curiosity were available to him because of his family's wealth and the wealth he himself was able to amass primarily because of his family's standing and fortune. As close as any other American to being a "Renaissance man," Jefferson no doubt was; but he was in a position to be so above all because of his inherited social and material—not biological or intellectual—advantages.

Like his mentor Jefferson, Madison too was born to wealth and social distinction and attended one of the nation's great and prestigious universities. Trained for the law but unwilling to practice it, Madison could live off his inherited estates and real estate speculation at a time in his early career when political offices in Virginia fell like ripe plums to young men of eminent family such as his. As he was to show at the Constitutional Convention in the spring of 1787 and in the *Federalist* papers that he, Alexander

Hamilton, and John Jay wrote shortly afterwards, Madison was not only a brilliant student of political theory and philosophy, but an original and penetrating contributor to the art. What enabled him to demonstrate his gifts was an early public career that was almost automatically conferred on him because of his family's standing rather than because of an innate capacity that he had not yet had time to reveal.

As the son of one of the nation's leading men, John Quincy Adams had an unexcelled education. As a young lawyer, after graduating from Harvard, the younger Adams slid easily into public service and did so primarily because his father was vice-president to George Washington. Even before his father had risen to second place in the nation, he had provided his son with invaluable political responsibilities and opportunities. Quincy Adams performed well, of course, demonstrating a forthrightness of character as well as acuity of mind that doubtless would have stood out in any context. Yet it could be said of him, as of his brilliant predecessors in the White House, that inherited social advantages, not individual promise, provided the catalyst for his crucially important start.

Although I have challenged James Bryce's observation that most presidents were men of humble or ordinary beginnings, who rose to the nation's highest office primarily because of their own "merits," I have no quarrel with his equally famous dictum that few great men have been elected president—or been selected as candidates for the presidency. (However, as I shall disclose in the concluding chapter, I have come to the same conclusion as he for different reasons.) Certainly few among the presidents exhibited great mental prowess in their earlier careers and, as I shall argue shortly, even fewer demonstrated unusually admirable traits of character. After the administration of John Quincy Adams, almost a century passed before another man of unusual intellectual distinction, Lincoln aside, was elected to the highest office. And this man, William Howard Taft, was quick to admit that he attributed his political success above all to his "father's prominence." His comment was a sign of honesty, not excessive modesty. Taft did brilliantly as a student at Yale but he could attend that great university because of his father's wealth and standing. When he graduated from law school, he could look forward to an "ensured position" not because of any Blackstonean precociousness he had demonstrated but because he was his father's son. High judicial, administrative, and political offices subsequently beckoned, largely because of the impressiveness of his own performance. A significant and intrinsic part of that performance was a philosophical conservatism congenial to the propertied men who financed and helped run the Republican party. And for all his powers of intellect and his capacity for hard work, Taft, as he himself knew, was able to play the political part he did, on center stage, above all because of his father's prominence.

Life being as perverse as it is—or perhaps it would be more precise to say, political success in America being as little dependent on great intellect as it is— Taft's presidency was hardly a dazzling one, by whatever standard, and was as a result confined to one term. The last of the truly brilliant men in the White House—at least by my standards—followed immediately after Taft. Although *his* performance was successful enough to assure his reelection, many people have wondered just how, finally, to evaluate Woodrow Wilson's two terms. Some are sour enough to think that nothing casts greater doubt on the wisdom of Plato's advice that, ideally, philosopher-statesmen should govern than Woodrow Wilson's performance, particularly in his second term. (In fairness to Plato, it must be noted that Wilson's obvious interest in winning the coveted office would have disqualified him for it in Plato's ideal republic.) Wilson first was an outstanding student and then an outstanding scholar, belonging to that very select circle whose first book remains important a century after its publication and does so for the light it throws on its subject, congressional government, rather than for the light it throws on its author—as is true of a number of books attributed to presidents. Nor in Wilson's case can there be any doubt that he is the actual and sole author of the many books published under his name. As the son of a prominent minister, Wilson did have the rare opportunity to study at the finest universities in the north and southeast. In view of his own achievements, it does seem fair to conclude that for Wilson even more than for his few predecessors in the White House who appear to have been men of unusually high intelligence, his greatest debt to his parents was for an inheritance of intellectual rather than material or social gifts.

Some might find it a sad commentary that not one among Wilson's successors over the past sixty-odd years could lay claim to great intellect. Others might demur, noting that, on the one hand, the presidential performance of the brilliant is mixed and that, on the other hand, the greatest success in administering the presidency depends less on brilliance than on other traits. Of course, there is brilliance and brilliance. Lincoln's is not associated with book learning as are Jefferson's, Madison's, the Adams's, and Wilson's; that fact may help explain the sagacity and the rare wisdom the sixteenth president displayed during his occupation of the high office.

If not brilliance, several of fortune's favorites did display traits of character and personality that combined with family affluence and influence to pave their way to the White House. As the skeptics and revisionists delight in pointing out, George Washington lost more battles than he won during the American Revolution. And yet despite his faults in military tactics and his limitations of temperament and intellect, Washington's resoluteness was the rock upon which an independent United States was built. Washington's steadfast character turned out to be a great unanticipated bonus to the new nation. But he was selected to serve as commander in chief of the armies not so much for his personal traits as for his great wealth, his aristocratic standing, what might be called his conservative "southernness," and for a prior modest experience of military leadership that only a man of his social eminence could have had. If Washington belonged to that elite class which, by virtue of its vast land and slave holdings, enjoyed a lavish lifestyle featured by splendid homes, costly furnishings and entertainment, and regular riding to the hounds, and which monopolized influential positions whether in the church, government, or militia, he did so because he was born to that class and inherited the properties necessary to membership in it. For him as for other presidents, marriage dramatically increased his wealth and standing. As I shall try shortly to show, his own privileged birth had much to do with his attractiveness as a marital partner to a woman of means and standing.

John Tyler's brief tenure as president is regarded by most historians as a failure, since he succeeded above all in alienating his own party and dooming his chances for nomination to what would have been his first full term. Yet his failure appears to have been due mainly to his integrity, or what contemporary critics called his stubbornness and betrayal in refusing to go along with a party program he could not in good conscience support. The Tyler character had been on display a few years earlier, when he resigned his seat in the U.S. Senate over an issue of political principle. Tyler had been selected by the Virginia state legislature for the Senate in the first instance, as earlier he had been chosen for the national House of Representatives and diverse high offices in Virginia, because he belonged to one of the Old Dominion's most eminent families. Tyler was a man of whom it was said that he had to expend no effort in social climbing for he was in the elite already. To all practical purposes, his lucrative legal practice, like his political career, were also simply his for the taking. All that was evidently required of the young Tyler to fall into these good things was freedom from glaring congenital deficiencies rather than exceptional promise of any sort. This is not to say that he was not capable, only that he does not appear to have been outstanding.

The best biography of Grover Cleveland is subtitled *A Study in Courage.* Both as mayor of Buffalo and as president of the United States, Cleveland demonstrated whatever courage was necessary to steer an independent course that on some issues put him at odds with legislators. He was, however, not above avoiding military service in the Civil War by hiring a substitute. Whatever part his well-publicized show of independence as local official may have played in ingratiating him with national party chieftains and the national electorate, there can be no doubt that his family connections significantly promoted both his private and public careers. When he began his legal career by working as a law clerk, he did so with one of the most prestigious firms in the Buffalo area, finding its doors open to him only because of the influence of his wealthy uncle. The blossoming of both his legal and political careers owed something to Cleveland's good sense, work habits, and conservatism but it owed a great deal too to the head start his uncle's connections had given him.

Nineteenth-century politicians were prone to speak of a presidential candidate's "availability," meaning by the term his realistic chances of winning his party's nomination and subsequently of achieving electoral success, in addition to his willingness to run. While no doubt sensitive to attractive traits of personality that might add to a man's appeal to voters, party managers did not make very much of this facet of candidacy—as is made clear by a listing of the lackluster personalities the major parties nominated during the century. In that perhaps fortunate era, the term *charisma* was unknown and not a factor in considering qualifications for high office. In the twentieth century, the term *availability* has gone out of fashion, replaced by the unspoken concept, "winnability." In this age of mass communications, a central ingredient of the latter concept has been a candidate's personal style, variously described as personality, charm, charisma, and human appeal, among other terms. Four presidents who rank very high by this criterion were Theodore Roosevelt, Franklin D. Roosevelt, John F. Kennedy, and Ronald Reagan.

I have already discussed Reagan under a different heading. Since his (first?) term is only slightly more than half completed at the time of writing, it is not altogether clear whether the historians' consensus will eventually judge him a successful as well as popular president. But for the other three charismatic leaders there seems little doubt: they are ranked in the upper echelon of American presidents. To judge from their performance in the White House (or from popular perceptions of that performance), attractive personality is neither an indication of lack of capacity nor a hindrance to substantial achievement. It need hardly be added in the case of these men that each of them rose quickly in politics for reasons having little to do either with his charm or ability and almost everything to do with the standing or the wealth and influence of his family.

When TR let it be known that he wished to be of the "governing class," he had no difficulty in being accommodated. As one of his biographers notes, had Roosevelt's "background been different . . . he would not even have been nominated for the legislature in the autumn of 1881." Other young men equally ambitious, promising, and gifted but lacking his wealth and connections, never realized their dream. Roosevelt's performance in a series of seemingly modest if not humdrum offices, his heroism as leader of the "Rough Riders," his attractive versatility and his wide interests all testified to his energy and ability. And yet his ample purse strings played a crucial part even in these matters, permitting him to shrug off low salaries that might have induced a poorer man to turn aside from such positions, to indulge his literary tastes, to be in a position to command what was in effect a private cavalry regiment, and to publicize these and other activities.

Born and raised amidst surroundings as elegant, a lifestyle as lavish, and opportunities as rare as those available to the "Republican Roosevelt," FDR had as little difficulty as his cousin in entering politics and quickly winning a success that appears to have been due above all to his family's name and standing. The Democratic Roosevelt does not appear to have talked of entering the governing class but, like TR, became one of their number merely by indicating his wish to do so. It was not every state assemblyman who, after one two-year term and a fraction of another, could be named assistant secretary of the navy and when that stint was completed, become the vice-presidential candidate of a major party. FDR did turn out to be an able and surprisingly humane governor during the early depression years and an even more remarkable and gifted leader during his long tenure in the White House. Perhaps fate has chosen to be kind to America during its darkest hours by providing us with exceptional leadership during the Civil War and the Great Depression. Yet for all his qualities of leadership, the fact remains that Franklin Roosevelt won the opportunity to display them above all because of the quality of his family name.

Kennedy's political success, unlike that of the two Roosevelts, can not be credited to family eminence. For the Kennedys could not lay claim to a standing equal to that attained by the old New York Dutch family. But the Kennedys did have great wealth and JFK's career benefited immensely from his father's readiness to dip into it in order to promote his son's political chances. Kennedy's highly publicized wartime exploits no doubt enhanced his image as political candidate, and his performance in office after each of his elections was, at worst, not an embarrassment. Every one of these elections was assured by the spending of sums that dwarfed the expenditures of his opponents, whether in Democratic primary contests or in the elections contested by Republicans. Before the presidential election of 1960, Kennedy's father indeed sold him "like soap flakes," realizing by these tactics the family's great political dream. John F. Kennedy was a most attractive candidate, as he was in some respects an appealing person. There can, however, be little question that his attractiveness and appeal to voters owed a great deal to a public image that was largely the product of a heavily financed media blitz.

Most of the remaining presidents, while beneficiaries all of important social and economic family advantages, had shown themselves to be capable men, whether in politics, business, or the military and legal professions. William Henry Harrison's chief claim to fame was his exploits as Indian fighter and general during the War of 1812. Some later military experts, like some of his contemporaries, have caviled, suggesting that his abilities and achievements were highly exaggerated. Certainly the Whig party put them to good propagandistic use during the presidential campaign of 1840. Whatever the final assessment of his military capacity may be, Harrison's career clearly was furthered by the mere fact of his family name. Particularly noteworthy was an event at the very outset of that career, after the young Harrison had decided to pass up the opportunity of studying medicine under the great Benjamin Rush. Passing over—and angering—men older and more experienced than Harrison, Governor Richard Henry Lee commissioned him an infantry ensign on no other ground than his membership in the First Families of Virginia. An explanation of Polk's meteoric rise in law and politics must be compounded of his ambition, his ability, and a closeness to Tennessee's leading men that appears to have been due mainly to his family's prominence and to his own activities as public man that stemmed from that prominence. Zachary Taylor won a great national reputation as old "Rough and Ready" for his campaigns in the Mexican War. Son of a wealthy and eminent planter and slaveowner, Taylor himself became a large landowner of ample means. And when as a young man he elected to follow a military career, his family's elite standing assured that he would pursue it from the officer class. Buchanan's rise to the presidency following a long career in national politics can be traced in part, obviously, to his performance as a reliable Democratic party stalwart, but his political success also owed a great deal to his profitable law practice. And that practice was a success almost from the outset because Buchanan, in common with many of his fortunate predecessors, was tutored for the law after graduating from college by one of the leading attorneys in the state, as befitted the son of an influential father.

William McKinley's prepresidential career, first as lawyer and then as congressman from and governor of Ohio, betrayed few if any signs either of unusual legal acumen or remarkable powers of statecraft. It was a career abetted by McKinley's steady habits, his comforting conservatism, his honorable service in the Civil War, and his unusually good education first at a private academy, then at college, and finally at law school. Warren G. Harding's was to a large extent a self-made career, the product of his "presidential looks," an appearance that made him attractive to impressionable women, the sound views that made him appealing to conservative businessmen, an ability to play the political game, and his artful promotion and expansion of the local newspaper he owned. His start in the newspaper business was made possible, of course, by the fact that his father was half-owner of the *Daily Star*, as his enrollment at college was made possible by the fact that his father was a successful doctor and businessman. Coolidge's career followed what was a recurrent pattern for American presidents: modest and growing success in law that paved the way for entry into local politics (in Coolidge's case, his senior law partners actually recruited him into political service) preceded by the kind of unusually good education that was available only to sons of prosperous men. Coolidge thus attended an exclusive private school, an excellent college, and then read for the law with men of unusual standing. Shortly before the Republican party named him as Harding's running mate in 1920, Coolidge gained immediate national prominence by his actions as governor of Massachusetts during the Boston police strike. It seems doubtful that he would have attained this position without the modest but crucial head start his father's position made possible. Jimmy Carter's reputation for great intelligence has been cultivated by some former members of his staff but it is not borne out by his actions in office, his public statements, and least of all by his autobiographical book, *Why Not the Best?* (If that volume represents Carter's idea of putting his best foot forward, interesting questions are raised about his standards of excellence.) Carter rose high in Georgia politics because he had been a successful businessman, and he was a successful businessman largely because he inherited a relatively substantial business that had been created by his father. Carter appears to have been a good naval officer as earlier he had evidently been a good student at the U.S. Naval Academy and before that at a junior college. But nothing about his intellectual efforts and promise appears to have had as much influence on his career as did the opportunities his father conferred on him.

A final group of presidents—Monroe, Pierce, Hayes, Arthur, and Benjamin Harrison—were in my judgment men of such modest personal attainments that if they had been deprived of their youthful family advantages they would have been bereft of whatever success they managed to achieve. Since such a judgment is based on an unavoidably subjective interpretation of partial evidence, it is bound to be challenged. Less controversial is the observation that each of these men was indebted to his advantageous early circumstances.

True, Monroe was intensely ambitious. But how much could the most driving personal ambition have done for him had he not been his father's and—even more significant— his mother's son and therefore nephew to the learned, eminent, and influential

Judge Joseph Jones? Had he not read for the law with Thomas Jefferson himself? Had he not accumulated vast acreage through speculation with funds made available to him by his inheritance? Had his wealth and eminence not made him an appropriate suitor to a woman belonging to one of New York's most prestigious families? Had his career not been regularly promoted by some of the nation's most powerful men—men who took an interest in this ambitious aristocrat for reasons that appear to have had little to do with his own personal traits of intellect or character?

Pierce had the unusually good private school and college education to be expected of the son of a man who was to become state governor, and he made the kind of socially advantageous marriage that family circumstances such as his made possible. Although he accomplished little in state politics and even less in the U.S. Senate, his political career blossomed nevertheless; although he revealed little aptitude for legal theory, his practice thrived financially. His success both in politics and law appears to have been due primarily to family influence and connections. He did have a war record but it was hardly a glorious one, since he saw no action. Yet nothing could impede the upward rush of his legal fees and his fame.

The chief element in Hayes's success appears to have been his rich and influential uncle, Sardis Birchard, who saw to it first that Hayes had an excellent education, through Harvard Law School, and then that his legal and political careers were launched auspiciously. A wounded hero of the Civil War and a loyal Republican who was seemingly ready to subordinate personal interests to the needs of the party, Hayes experienced little difficulty in rising to the pinnacle of state politics. Since the state was Ohio—the politically blessed province where late-nineteenth- and early twentieth-century presidents were made—Hayes had as little difficulty in becoming the head of the nation.

For a century American schoolchildren have been taught that Chester A. Arthur turned over a new leaf as president—one more example of the fact that the highest office brings out the best in a man—after an earlier career that was admittedly a cross between mundane and sordid. The most hard-boiled amoralists were said to have blanched at the prospect of Chet Arthur in the White

House, their long-submerged patriotism somehow resurrected at the dread thought of a man so low occupying a place so high. In fairness to Arthur, he was not merely a passive beneficiary of good fortune. His own unremitting ambition, opportunism, shrewdness, sybaritism, egotism, and conservatism had much to do with his splendid political successes. Among other things, he saw to it that he was not shot at during the Civil War. Perhaps Arthur is more appropriately placed among those presidents who, while depending to a large extent on early family advantages, nevertheless rose as high as they did primarily because of their own efforts, for good or for ill. As the child of a successful man, Arthur did receive that private school and college education and the opportunity to become a lawyer that was so rare a pattern for the American people in the nineteenth century but so common a pattern in the lives of the presidents.

That leaves Benjamin Harrison, the example par excellence of a man of the most modest attributes and achievements who yet, as the grandson of a great eminence— in this case of a president of the United States—found one door after another opening up for him, enabling him to rise to ever higher levels of political prestige, almost entirely because of the political magic in his family name. It is hard to say whether it was his father's cash or contacts that proved more helpful in furthering both Harrison's legal and political careers. Like other courageous young men of his time, he saw heavy action in the Civil War but unlike most of them, he saw it not as an enlisted man but as an officer. Like Taft after him, Harrison was quick to concede that he owed his increasingly good fortune above all to his father's influence. Unlike Taft, however, Harrison was himself a man of modest talents. When someone later, no doubt appalled at the discrepancy between the ideal qualifications for the highest office and those Harrison brought to it, called him the little man in the big chair, he was not being unfair except, alas, in singling out Benjamin Harrison for a harsh evaluation that could with equal justice have been made about some of those who preceded and followed him in the White House.

In trying to assess the influence of the presidents' origins on their adult careers, something must be said, I think, about their marriages. Most of the presidents made what society calls "good" or socially or economically advantageous marriages well before they occupied the White House. (Interestingly, the only presidents who married into families lower on the social scale than their own are three of the most recent—Nixon, Ford, and Carter.) Nor can there be any question but that a number of these good marriages played an important role in advancing the careers of the men who made them. In view of the fact that Buchanan was the only president who never married, it might be argued that the American public expects its presidents to be—or, like the widowers among them, to have been—married men, in a sense making all the presidents' marriages *politically* advantageous. In this discussion, my interest is only in marriages that significantly promoted a man's career and in those good marriages that appear to have owed something to the presidents' own early standing.

Lincoln made what was a classic good marriage, marrying a woman of truly aristocratic family and by this union enhancing his own social standing and solidifying his position among the professional and political elite of his community. (The actual misery this marriage inflicted on Lincoln demonstrates only that a "good marriage" is not necessarily the same thing as a happy marriage.) Whatever the sources of Lincoln's attractiveness to Mary Todd may have been, they could not have included family eminence. A similar point might be made about Ronald Reagan's marriage to Nancy Davis, while granting that the Davises did not occupy so high a social plateau as the Todds. But since socially advantageous and even socially upward marriages that owed nothing to the prestige or wealth of the presidents' families are not truly germane to this discussion, the marriages of Lincoln and Reagan shall not be further considered and the good marriages made by Fillmore, Garfield, and Eisenhower shall be passed over.

In examining the role of social and economic standing in the presidents' marriages, it is not my intention to dismiss the part that might have been played by sentimental and romantic feelings. We are here speaking of motives, always elusive and beyond the power of researchers to get at, no matter how arduously they try. Letters written by shrewd and even by considerate men to fiancées for whom they feel no burning ardor are likely nevertheless to speak the language of love. In contrast, seemingly cold letters written by shy men and women guided by Victorian ideals of seemliness may mask strong emotions. With men and women as complex as they are, passionate feelings may commingle with cool appraisals of self-interest. All of which is to say that trying to understand why anyone chooses a particular marital partner is no less difficult than trying to understand his or her motives in doing anything else. Sophisticated statisticians report that no statistical procedure has yet been devised to explain why anyone does anything. Since such novelists as Jane Austen or Balzac were the creators of their fictional heroes and heroines, they like God could speak with assurance of the motives underlying the marriages made by the characters they had created. Mere historians, lacking omniscience, can only guess at or infer what was on the minds of their nonfictional actors. They do well enough, it seems to me, if their guesses and inferences are informed and sensible.

In the absence of "smoking gun" evidence on the motives of the men and women who entered into "presidential marriages," there is no alternative to making sensible inferences from the evidence. Fortunately, my interest is not in their motives but in their actions, for I am not arguing that certain presidents *sought* to marry well but only that they *did* marry well. To prove the former would require a close examination of motives. To prove the latter requires only evidence on the standing and circumstances of their brides and their brides' families.

True, my suggestion that the standing of the presidents' families did play a part in the good marriages that a number of them made does get at the motives of the women they married and the families they married into. Presumably, the bride and her parents consented in part because they looked with favor on the standing or circumstances of the future president. No one knows what was in the heart of hearts of the brides and their families. My earlier research on the marital behavior of thousands of members of the nineteenth-century social and economic elite revealed that almost without exception they married as if by a rule of social endogamy: swells married swells. Many sociological studies confirm the prevalence of this pattern. This is not to say that romance and passion played no part in these alliances. The evidence indicates rather that since the upper crust moved within a social world populated almost exclusively by their own sort, great ardor if and when it did erupt was directed toward a member of their own circle—as was the case, certainly, when Theodore Roosevelt fell in love with and married Alice Lee.

My working assumption is that in marriages between women of wealthy or prestigious family and presidents of similar background, the standing of the presidents' families was one of the considerations in the minds of their brides and the parents or relatives of their brides.

A number of the presidents helped maintain their high status by marrying women of roughly similar standing. This group includes Hayes in marrying Lucy Ware Webb of a Virginia and Kentucky slaveowning family; Taft in marrying Helen ("Nellie") Herron, of a family of "substance and intelligence"; Wilson in marrying Ellen Louise Axson (another unquestionable love match), the daughter of a prominent minister who was a friend and peer of Wilson's father; Coolidge in marrying Grace Goodhue, a college graduate and daughter of an old New England family; and Franklin D. Roosevelt in marrying his cousin Eleanor Roosevelt.

Others made marriages that, if they added no luster to their standing, were nevertheless good marriages in not impairing—certainly not significantly detracting from—that standing. Dolley Payne Todd Madison's father did not thrive too well but only because of his Quaker convictions. The Paynes were a "substantial" Virginia slaveowning family. Madison's wife was the widow of a young lawyer who moved in the highest social circles of Philadelphia Quaker society before he fell victim to the cholera epidemic of 1793. John Quincy Adams married Louisa Catherine Johnson, whose uncle was the Governor of Maryland and whose father was a substantial merchant. Van Buren's wife Hannah Hoes was a relative of his mother and a childhood playmate. (That Van Buren, like several other presidents, was a widower before he moved into the White House evidently had no negative effect either on the calculations of party managers or the American electorate; it was enough that he *had* been married.) Zachary Taylor married Margaret Mackall Smith of a prominent Maryland family that had come to this country in the seventeenth century; her great-great-grandfather had been attorney general of Maryland at the time Oliver Cromwell ruled England. The family of Carrie Scott was not as luminous socially as that of her husband Benjamin Harrison but her father, the Reverend Dr. John W. Scott, is described by a Harrison biographer as "somewhat of a pioneer in the field of education for women," having organized a college for women. Grover Cleveland's marriage to Frances Folsom, the young daughter of a long time intimate, did not take place until he was into his first term. (Cleveland's well-publicized earlier illicit relationship with a woman left no doubt about his "manliness.")

Several of the presidents, although born to families of high standing, were able to raise their own status slightly but not insignificantly because of the still loftier status of the families of the women they married. With John Adams's marriage to Abigail Smith, "a strain of aristocracy was . . . introduced into the Adams line," for this daughter of Rev. William and Elizabeth Quincy Smith was descended of Quincys and Nortons, families traceable back to the time of William the Conqueror. James Monroe's daughter could be sought after by Samuel Gouverneur, a rich lawyer of a most prestigious New York City family, because Monroe's wife was Elizabeth Kortright, daughter of a New York family of similar eminence—a family bound through marriage with the Gouverneurs, Crugers, Quackenbosses, and other elite families in New York and other cities along the eastern seaboard. In the phrase of a biographer, Andrew Jackson "surely knew" that his marriage to Rachel Donelson Robards was socially advantageous. Her father had perhaps one social peer in all of Tennessee (and it was *not* Jackson) and in Virginia had been a friend of George Washington, a vestryman, lieutenant colonel in the militia, and several times a member of the House of Burgesses—activities all that stamped him a member of the elite. An emotional man who evidently felt a strong passion for his wife, Jackson married her even before her divorce from her first husband was completed. She in her turn had reason to know of Jackson's increasingly high standing in Tennessee society.

In marrying Jane Means Appleton, daughter of the late president of Bowdoin College, Franklin Pierce was now bound to a family with "substantial and aristocratic connections" in New England, one which, because of its numerous intermarriages with patrician lineages, occupied a higher social level than his own. Grant's father was a successful man but he could not match the social luster of the future president's father-in-law, Col. Frederick Dent. Julia Dent's father was a slaveowning member of a family earlier in the Maryland "aristocracy" who, by the time of Julia's marriage to Grant, were in the circle of the "best families in St. Louis." Harry Truman's wife, Elizabeth Virginia ("Bess") Wallace, was born into the "aristocracy" of Independence, Missouri. Her grandfather George Gates had made a fortune in flour milling, becoming a "pillar of the Independence social set," and living in a style befitting his high status. Although her parents could not match Gates's success, Miss Wallace evidently never lost her sense of being of the elite and she could in fact look forward to an impressive bequest when her parents died. Jackie Lee Bouvier's family was not as rich as John Kennedy's but its social standing was surely higher, as, for that matter, was the standing of her stepfather Hugh Auchincloss. Lyndon Johnson's wife, Claudia Taylor, was the daughter of Thomas Taylor, a successful, largely self-made businessman, and Minnie Patillo Taylor, whose father owned a large plantation in Alabama. If LBJ seemed intent on marrying a woman whose father was the richest man in his community, this particular woman appears to have been excited by his political promise as well as by his person. Certainly the marriage paid off for Johnson, not least in the literal sense.

It was impossible, given the upper-crust status of their families, for Washington, Jefferson, or William Henry Harrison to enhance their social standing by marriage. But they could and did improve their economic circumstances through matrimony. Martha Washington's father, Col. John W. Dandridge, was a rich and prominent Tidewater planter who provided his daughter with what a biographer calls "the best social credentials [in] the most tightly held, elite aristocracy in the colonies." Perhaps more to the point, she was the widow of Daniel Parke Custis, only son to the richest man in his Tidewater county. When he died, he left his widow a vast estate that made her one of the richest single women in Virginia. When a year and a half later Washington married her, he vaulted into "another economic sphere," more than doubling his already substantial properties. It may be, as one historian has written, that Washington's awareness that he had "acquired most of his holdings through marriage was an irritant to his pride." But it was a great stimulant to his pocketbook. Not directly germane but of interest nevertheless is the absence from Washington's whirlwind courtship of this wealthy widow of the ardor he earlier had displayed, say, for Miss Sally Fairfax.

Like his great predecessor, Jefferson too married a young woman whose social credentials were impeccable but whose wealth was perhaps even more interesting to him. Two years after she married Jefferson, Martha Wayles Skelton inherited 135 slaves and more than 11,000 acres, with one stroke more than doubling her husband's wealth and "ease of circumstances." True, the debts surrounding the inheritance would later plague Jefferson. However, he entered into the partnership with open eyes, fully "aware of the fact that [his intended] belonged to a wealthy family." Certainly his economic windfall, coming as it did just before the War of Independence, enabled him in the period that followed to focus all his energies on statecraft, public service, acquiring yet more knowledge, and the sybaritic living that his greatest biographer concedes was so vital to the happiness of his great subject.

By the time William Henry Harrison married Anna Symmes, his own somewhat disappointing career had so tarnished his family name that the bride's father stayed away from the wedding, despite consenting to it, out of unhappiness with his daughter's choice. Judge John Cleve Symmes was an extremely rich landowner and land speculator, who for twenty-five years had been chief justice of the Northwest Territory. The marriage did much to enhance Harrison's constant search for the good life—a concept, need it be said, that to him was represented by material, not spiritual, rewards.

Polk may have profited socially as well as economically in marrying Sarah Childress, who is described by a Polk biographer as no beauty but something of a "catch." Her father Joel Childress was a man of large and diverse business interests, a wealthy planter living in a splendidly furnished big house in which he entertained Tennessee's elite. Childress left a "munificent estate" and his daughter's wedding to Polk was a "major social event" in Tennessee. The McKinleys and Hoovers did, as upper-middle-class families, command some respect. As was true of the Southerners, McKinley and Hoover through marriage abetted perhaps slightly their prestige and even more clearly their financial circumstances. McKinley's wife Ida Paxton was the daughter of a wealthy banker and businessman. Her inheritance would take a great deal of financial pressure off McKinley. Sadly, her long illness, contracted within two years of the wedding, made life difficult, while her "luxurious" tastes ate into her fortune. But expenses notwithstanding, it seems clear that the marriage enabled McKinley subsequently to turn down a lavish income if the job did not interest him. Hoover married a friend of his college days, Lou Henry, who, like McKinley's wife, was the daughter of a bank president. Her father Charles Delano Henry, an Ohio Episcopalian, had moved to California where he founded and headed several banks and was thus in a position to leave a large estate to his only daughter. At the time of the marriage Hoover, although on the verge of becoming rich, had not yet attained that fortunate status. Wilson's second wife, Edith Bolling Gault, was, as the widow of a successful jewelry shop owner, probably wealthier than Wilson, and she came of an old Virginia family that in its better days no doubt had a social standing close to his own. This marriage took place after Wilson had entered the White House, but it did precede his reelection.

Finally, there is a group of presidents whose marriages were resoundingly advantageous both socially and financially. His biographer reports that John Tyler betrayed none of the ardor of youth at any time during his courtship of Letitia Christian, not even on the day of his wedding. Why, then, did he marry her? The answer may lie in the fact that the marriage was "a means of promoting his professional and political ambitions, as it strengthened his connections with the influential families of the Peninsula," in Virginia. The Christians were a prominent family with many connections; the bride's father was a man of "considerable property and influence," and the estate he left his daughter shortly after the marriage proved invaluable to young Tyler. (Although Letitia Tyler was later invalided, fortunately for her peace of mind her husband "betrayed" enough ardor after marriage for the couple to have nine children.) The widower Tyler's marriage, near the end of his one term in the White House, to his second wife, the beauteous and socially prominent Julia Gardiner, was a marriage that had no effect, obviously, on his prepresidential career.

Chester Arthur married Ellen Lewis ("Nell") Herndon, whose father Captain William Lewis Herndon was the distinguished son of a distinguished Virginia family, traceable back to the seventeenth century, and whose great-grandfather on the maternal side, General Hugh Mercer, "raised the first Virginia regiment in the American Revolution." Her mother was the former Elizabeth Frances Hansbrough of an aristocratic Southern family and a woman active in Washington's "best society." Adding to the pleasure-loving Arthur's joy was the fact that he and his bride were able to move into his mother-in-law's fashionable New York City house shortly after the marriage.

Warren Harding's wife may not have favorably impressed the second Mrs. Wilson, whom she replaced as first lady. But to her husband, says one of Harding's biographers, Florence Mabel Kling represented "the pinnacle of that small-town world [of Marion, Ohio]: wealth, position, assurance. Through her he could foresee the acceptance that had been denied him. He never loved her, but he did not say no to her." True, she had been another man's wife in what might have been a shotgun marriage—in view of her "condition." True, also, her father did not even talk to her at the time Harding married her. Ah, but her father was the richest man in town and he might yet—and he did—come around. It may not have been a marriage made in heaven but at least it immediately provided Harding with a wife who turned out to be a marvelously effective co-worker on the newspaper through which he built his fortune and his political career.

To what extent was the great success achieved by almost all the presidents in their prepresidential careers due to the privileged birth and upbringing most of them enjoyed? The answer seems clear: to a very great extent.

The unusually favorable circumstances in which most of the presidents began life gave them a distinct advantage over most Americans in the struggle for success. Although a few of them were blessed with an intelligence so great or a personality so impressive that it seems likely they would have made their mark even in the absence of their inherited material and social advantages, the great majority appear to have been something less than extraordinary in their native intellect and character. Inordinate ambition does seem to have been common among them. The problem with such ambition as an explanation of worldly success, however, is that it seems likely that many people who fell by the wayside did so despite great ambition.

The presidents' favorable starting points in some cases gave them slight but significant advantages, as when it provided access to higher education and to professional training that for most of American history were beyond the reach of 98 or 99 out of 100 contemporaries of theirs. And when they prepared for the law, the relative renown of their families attracted to them mentors with the prestige and influence that open up the inside track, which in turn separates the outstanding professionals from the common run of practitioners. In other cases the presidents' youthful advantages were so great that achieving great wealth, professional stature, high political office, or a combination of these attractive social destinations seems to have required little more of them than that they be something other than imbecile or depraved.

Worldly plums, like socially attractive wives, appear to have fallen into the laps of most of them more because of who they were than because of what they were. Their favored origins may have been a matter of indifference to the parties that later nominated them to the presidency. Yet these advantageous beginnings were precisely what enabled most of the presidents to become viable candidates, capable of catching the eye of party managers and nominating conventions.

☆☆☆☆☆ CHAPTER SIX ☆☆☆☆☆

What Does It All Signify?

MOST OF THE PRESIDENTS were born to families at or near the top of the American social and economic order. And abetted by their youthful advantages, they forged successful prepresidential careers and made good marriages that further widened the gulf between the leaders and the led in America. The great question is, what is the significance of the presidents' early and later advantages? What does their unrepresentativeness or atypicality tell us about American politics, American society, American values?

Clearly the evidence contradicts a number of enduring and widespread myths.

Despite what generations of writers, politicians, and orators have said to the contrary, poor boys have rarely risen to the top of the heap in this country. For most of American history, children born to the rural and urban working classes were simply unable to secure the higher education and the subsequent professional training that were necessary to pave the way to high political office. Some youngsters were of course able to surmount all barriers and achieve great distinction, but their numbers were never legion. The comparatively few American presidents who were born to families of modest station only match the small proportion of the nation's rich and successful who started at or near the bottom of the social ladder. The venerable American dream that any boy can rise to the presidency if he displays what James Bryce called the necessary "merit" turns out to be an illusion—unless merit is redefined to mean having parents and grandparents whose standing, wealth, and influence help open the doors to success in life. The difficult early circumstances of Andrew Johnson, James Garfield, Millard Fillmore, and Richard Nixon were only the exceptions that help prove the rule: the political race here as elsewhere has usually been won by those who had the advantage of starting from a favorable position.

Interestingly, this appears to have been so not because the major party managers and those influential at party nominating conventions are or were prejudiced against candidates who were poor boys. Far from it. All things being equal, political kingmakers in America would have been delighted had they been able to select presidential candidates born to poverty or to modest circumstances. For shrewd wire-pullers are quite aware of the political appeal in candidates of plebeian origins. The incessant poor-mouthing of their boyhoods by rich and successful Americans testifies to their awareness of the political capital that can be derived from humble beginnings.

Paradoxically, the major parties that have since George Washington's time exercised a monopoly over the selection of presidents have had little real interest in the actual early circumstances of their candidates for the presidency—for all their understanding of the political profit lurking in early circumstances that were in fact dismal or that can be portrayed as dismal. The chief interest of the parties appears to have been focused on what I would call the ideological soundness of their candidates for the nation's highest office. The common characteristic of the golden thirty-nine who have occupied the highest office, for all their dissimilarities in other respects, has been the essential conservatism of their social, economic, and political beliefs. Some had achieved great wealth before they were chosen, most had accumulated ample if less than dazzling fortunes. But all of them were champions of the prevailing order.

There is a school of thought which, observing that political leaders are drawn almost invariably from the higher levels of the social structure, concludes that it is precisely their social and economic success that is their chief attraction to party managers. But if this were the case, would not all of the presidents and presidential candidates have been drawn from the very highest classes alone? Yet the parties occasionally dipped down into social levels that, while hardly low, were nevertheless not at the very apex of the social structure. In fact, of the sixteen men who have held the office in the twentieth century, only four belonged to the nation's very highest social echelon—the two Roosevelts, Taft, and Kennedy (whose status was fortified by his marriage). The others were of course successful men. But what they all had in common and shared with their predecessors were social beliefs that party chieftains found comforting.

The parties have tapped the "successful classes" for their highest leaders not out of a slavish devotion to the principle that the upper orders alone contain candidates who are suitable but rather because, in searching for men of the appropriately reliable social philosophy, they have found that such men were likely to be men who have thrived under American society's prevailing arrangements.

Were successful men in America as upwardly mobile as a long-popular myth claims they were, a fair share of the men who became presidents could be expected to have been born to poor or humble parents and families. Almost 150 years ago Alexis de Tocqueville's *Democracy in America* told us that most rich Americans had earlier been poor boys whose families had felt "the sting of want." Over the following generations, Horatio Alger and other publicists agreed that rags to riches continued to be the dominant motif in the career lines of successful Americans. But these cheerful findings of Tocqueville and later yea-sayers were based, essentially, on a quick glance at the surface of American society and on the assumption that Andrew Carnegie, John D. Rockefeller, and a handful of other highly publicized industrial magnates born to modest circumstances were typical of the rich. But they were not. Probing a great mass of evidence on the backgrounds of the wealthy and the successful, for all periods in American history, sociologists, historians, and other scholars have discovered that, in the memorable phrase of one economic historian, poor boys who became rich or successful business leaders "have always been more conspicuous in American history books than in American history." Very few began at or near the bottom. The lives of the presidents only illustrate this principle: Americans who attain great worldly success, whether in wealth and property accumulation, occupational prestige, or politics, have typically been born to youthful advantages that were instrumental in accounting for their adult success. That is why few of the presidents were poor boys. They reached the heights largely because of the significant boost given most of them at birth and during their youth.

The evidence signifies, too, that in selecting presidential candidates, the major parties have sought not the best men but safe men. That the parties' interest has not been in the best men is indicated by the almost palpable mediocrity of so many of the presidential candidates and—sad to say—so many of the presidents. Clearly, they could have chosen better had they wished to.

In a well-known chapter of his classic study, *The American Commonwealth*— "Why Great Men Are Not Chosen Presidents"— James Bryce argued that to the Republicans and Democrats, it was "more important that [their] nominee should be a good candidate than that he should turn out a good president." In what has become the conventional wisdom, the chief requirement of a major party candidate for the highest office is supposedly that he be a likely winner. But why then have the major parties so often presented the nation with lackluster candidates? Party political machinery, finances, and propaganda have proven quite capable of assuring the electorate that the sow's ear importuning their voting support was in reality a silk purse. But would the parties not have found it easier, cheaper, and more certain to assure victory had they insisted on candidates more attractive than those they have so often settled for?

Bryce astutely observed that American political life gave "fewer opportunities for personal distinction" than European and that in this country there was also a comparatively small "proportion of first-rate ability drawn into politics." Yet surely there were abler men, in politics and out, who could have been tapped for nomination to the highest office in preference to the unlikely individuals so often chosen, men as lacking in obvious popular appeal as they were lacking in intellectual distinction and high character.

The major parties do indeed love to win. That is why political scientists call them pragmatic parties. Numerous studies by historians and political scientists disclose that the policies and programs that have been hammered out by the major parties in the United States have been policies and programs that were not likely to rock the boat. More important to the parties than winning per se is winning with the right kind of candidate: a man of sound views. A great consolation to each major party is the knowledge that the mediocrity they at times put forward as standard bearer may not be at a competitive disadvantage, since their opponents select candidates by criteria similar to their own. Both parties have sought as presidential candidates not their best or even their most attractive men but the most attractive of the safe and sound men available to them. Presidential candidates have invariably been men who were earlier successful, not because the parties follow an inflexible rule requiring such a background but rather because the appropriate social ideology is most likely to be found among men in the upper social clusters. Nor have the parties left this crucial matter to chance or to the laws of statistical probability.

While men successful in worldly affairs are as a group likely to be conservative and sympathetic to the fundamental social and economic arrangements under which they have thrived, individuals among them may turn out to be mavericks or "traitors to their class." The historical record is sprinkled with evidence of high-minded persons born to great advantages, who devoted their lives to the unpopular cause of redressing the social imbalance. But such well-born radicals and social critics have always been in short supply. And they are altogether rare in those great opportunistic political coalitions—the American major parties.

Every single president had had a career that gave assurance of his acceptance of the prevailing social and economic order, whatever its inequities. The major parties have so often reached out for men of substantial political experience because these political careers could be closely scrutinized for the candidates' operative values and because these careers could disclose as well whether the candidates knew how to play the game. So many of the nominees have been lawyers not because presidents need to have the technical expertise in lawmaking that only legal training ensures but because lawyers are so often respectful of property rights and of the social and economic order built on these rights.

What I call the ideological soundness of the presidents is not contradicted by the fact that some of them have been more liberal than others or that the Democrats among them have been more willing than the Republican incumbents to reform the system or ameliorate some of its more glaring abuses. Democrats are and have been more likely to be responsive to the needs of economic—if, for a long time, not racial—have-nots than their Republican rivals. Only seven Democratic presidents have served since the Civil War. A much higher proportion of this small number were men of liberal reputation than is to be found among the seventeen Republicans who have held the high office over the same period. But Democratic presidents no less than Republican have been opposed to anything more than slight tinkering with the prevailing social order. As the political scientist Philip Burch has recently shown, whether of the one party or the other, whether purportedly liberal or conservative, American presidents almost without exception confine their choice of cabinet, judicial, and ambassadorial appointees to men who have been inordinately rich and successful. The reforms associated with FDR's New Deal have been denounced in some quarters as radical and even revolutionary. That these reforms were actually designed to preserve the system by protecting it against its own worst abuses and the consequence of these abuses is indicated by the fact that similar reforms had been introduced a half century earlier in Europe by the great conservatives Disraeli and Bismarck.

I do not mean to suggest that presidential—and vice-presidential—candidates have been selected in "smoke-filled rooms" or in nominating conventions according to a slide rule formula rigidly applied. The American political system is and has been flexible enough to permit chance and idiosyncratic factors, such as a strong personal dislike by influential wire-pullers to an otherwise unobjectionable contender, sometimes to determine who gets the nod, who is rejected. The fact remains that the major parties have invariably chosen relatively wealthy and successful men to head the ticket. They appear to have done so because it is from a pool of men such as these that "sound principles" are most likely to be found. And in view of the little movement from rags to riches that has actually occurred in American history, the great majority of these men were born to relatively prosperous and prestigious parents and families.

I have spoken of the conservative social views of the men who became president. Some admirers of Jefferson, Jackson, Lincoln, the two Roosevelts, Wilson, Truman, and perhaps Lyndon Johnson may wonder whether social conservatism truly describes the beliefs of these men. This is hardly the occasion for an extended discussion of the social philosophies of the American presidents. Yet even a less than exhaustive reading of their earlier and their presidential public addresses, writings, and private correspondence makes it quite clear that every one of them was devoted to the preservation of the prevailing social and economic order.

The willingness of Wilson and the Roosevelts to curb some monopolistic and antisocial business practices, to increase the extent of federal regulation of the economy, or to provide diverse but modest benefits to working people, the poor, and the underprivileged were in a great conservative tradition that sought, if anything, to strengthen the prevailing order by ridding or correcting it of its worst abuses. Wilson had no use for social radicals or radicalism. TR denounced what he called the "lunatic fringe" that favored drastic changes in the system and he branded as "muckrakers" reformers who dwelt excessively on society's sore spots. His views are an almost perfect example of the traditional conservative ideal of social paternalism, according to which the upper classes and the "governing class" help meet their responsibility in a society under which they have flourished by acting benevolently toward the mass of people on whom fortune has not smiled. Neither before nor after he became president did FDR evince the slightest interest in or sympathy for men and movements that would challenge the fundamental principles of the American capitalistic order. That some overwrought extremists described the reforms he favored as "socialistic" did not make them so. He spoke truth when he said he was no socialist but a friend, rather, to capitalism at a time when it was badly in need of strong medicine to restore it to health.

The record is similarly clear for the other presidents of liberal reputation. If Jefferson feared anything, it was a society governed or dominated by masses of the propertyless, avid to overhaul the social order in their own selfish interest. By his actions as by his utterances, Jackson displayed his lack of concern for the plight of debtors and his lack of interest in the problems of working people. A close study of his seven volumes of correspondence reveals that he mentioned "labor" perhaps five times. Like other conservative property owners before and after his time, he believed that rich and poor alike must be left to shift for themselves, with government offering neither protection nor advantages to any social group. The prepresidential Lincoln was no abolitionist or friend to abolitionists and, as president, he resisted the demand that slavery be ended, until midway in the great war he found it politically and militarily feasible to put an end to it—if at first on a piecemeal basis. For all his glorious rhetoric as to the virtue of free labor, he held to that conventional elitist belief that honest and virtuous working people would, if they were persistent, rise to the highest economic levels in American society; no substantial changes were needed in a social order so flexible, so appreciative of individual merit. LBJ's civil rights ideas are morally admirable but, as with Jackson, when his overheated electoral rhetoric is discounted, nothing in either his deeds or statements betrays any interest in changing society in the interests of those who are have-nots through no fault of their own. Much of his congressional career was devoted to behind-the-scenes manipulation that by hugely rewarding a few great capitalists only widened the economic gulf between haves and have-nots.

In the political democracy that is the United States, seekers after high elective office necessarily have to express their love of and great sympathy for the mass of ordinary voters. The harsh word for the more hypocritical versions of this form of populistic rhetoric is demagogy. In the informal political division of labor that has in effect been worked out over the past century, the Democratic party has characterized itself as the party of labor, marginal farmers, small business, ethnic—and since the era of the New Deal—racial as well as religious minorities. The Republicans have directed their appeal to the more prosperous elements in American society in general and big business in particular and to what was once the WASP majority, which has more recently become yet another minority. Inevitably, campaigns between parties such as these will produce rhetorical excesses in which one party denounces its opponents as "radicals" and "revolutionists," while the other party retaliates with the cry, "reactionary plutocrats" and "selfish aristocrats." Many Americans have no doubt been taken in by this fiery language. In fact, as Richard Hofstadter, William N. Chambers, and other students of American politics have observed, both parties have been dedicated to maintaining the status quo. They have taken some pains to confine candidacy for the nation's highest political office to men known to be sympathetic to its fundamental social, economic, and political arrangements. And they have searched for such men from among the upper levels of the prevailing order, where contentment with the way things are is most likely to reign.

Until the modern era, most of the presidents did not bother to conceal their conservative social biases. Monroe let his annoyance be shown at the very idea of a social inferior marrying someone who was her social better. Jackson favored a property qualification for officeholders. William Henry Harrison the presidential candidate was not averse to accepting large sums from great capitalists, making it "probable," according to a sympathetic biographer, that his behavior placed him under special obligations to these men. Fillmore also received lavish gifts from "grateful New York City monied men" in appreciation for his "sound" public performance. The solution to social problems, said Hayes before he was elected president, was "in the home, the school, the [lecture] platform, the pulpit, and the press"—everywhere, that is, but in governmental action. Garfield periodically reminded life's failures that their plight was due to their own deficiencies, not society's. Businessmen, we are told, liked Cleveland "because he was instinctively conservative." "American business," said Harding, "is not a monster but an expression of [a] God-given impulse to create, and the savior and the guardian of our happiness." Liberty to Harding, observes a critic, meant "liberty for the rich to become richer and the poor, if they were fortunate, to become rich." In Coolidge's version of the good society, labor's reward for hard work would be a modest standard of living and common schools for its children, while capitalists in contrast would live luxuriously and send their children to the great universities and on educational travel abroad. For all the recent attempts by some historians to portray the Hoover administration as a vigorous predecessor of the New Deal, the conservatism of Herbert Hoover's fundamental social and economic beliefs shines through the president's own efforts to camouflage them in his public rhetoric. Upper classes, he said, had been called by God to their lofty station. The greatest incentive to human progress was the profit motive. Labor and capital were not separate classes but groups of fellow producers. Private enterprise alone insured spiritual freedom. And in Hoover's unique definition, true social security meant above all the freedom to make profit through the beneficent operations of free enterprise.

Eisenhower after the war publicly bemoaned the penchant of too many Americans to depend on government handouts rather than on their own hard work. Working people, he said, should put aside unrealistic hopes for champagne and caviar and settle for beer and hot dogs. Given Ronald Reagan's sometime career as philosophical spokesman for General Electric, it is not surprising that the prepresidential record of no other chief executive is as heavily sprinkled with affirmations of the glory of "the system" and of his love for it. Told in 1950 by Ralph Cordiner, president of GE, to "get yourself a philosophy you can stand for and the country can stand for!", Reagan did just that, turning far rightward for the appropriate principles. Epitomizing his beliefs is the observation he once made to an interviewer that "one of the most dangerous slogans ever coined is 'the greatest good for the greatest number.'"

John Adams, Jefferson, Madison, and perhaps Wilson aside, these were not political philosophers or deep social thinkers. There is good reason to suspect that the public statements many of them made testify more to the public image they sought to cultivate than to their innermost beliefs. Probably their actual social beliefs are best inferred from their private and public actions, rather than searched for in their writings and speeches. In seeking to pursue the main chance as avidly as they all did, whether in war or peace, in business, politics, or law, they revealed their operative philosophy: the system was to be used and exploited for personal advantage, not transformed in accord with some heroic ideal. And as political men, whether before they reached the White House or after, every one of them showed himself to be a pragmatist—at least, of sorts. No social rebel or dissident is to be found lurking among the presidents.

The question in the context of this discussion is, of course, what was the influence of the presidents' early and later advantages on their working philosophies as political leaders? It is not an easy question to answer, since there is no way of measuring the precise effect of men's condition on their thinking. The belief that rich, conservative men are conservative because they are rich is very popular but it is not necessarily or invariably true.

Equally popular is the companion belief that people who are very well off are inevitably conservative. A nice example of such thinking is provided by a woman who described herself as a "rock-ribbed Republican." On March 5, 1977, she spoke on the telephone with President Carter during his "Call In" radio program. Referring to the president's plea for a thoroughgoing tax reform, the woman, Mrs. Esther Thomas of Villanova, Pennsylvania, asked, "How can we as middle-class wage earners expect legislation or reform that would remove tax loopholes the rich or affluent use as deductions, when all laws and legislation are made by the rich?" She continued, "There are no poor people, no lower-class wage earners in either House or the Senate." (Interestingly, the president's answer to Mrs. Thomas was so unresponsive that Walter Cronkite, the moderator, chided him for his evasiveness.) And not long ago, three well-known non-Marxist social scientists could actually write that "a person thinks, politically, as he is socially. Social characteristics determine political preference." But surely there are too many exceptions to justify accepting this as a rule!

We have learned that ideas and beliefs—including the social ideas and beliefs of the successful—are shaped not only by men's and women's material and social circumstances but by many other elements in their lives and in their own makeup. Ideas are shaped in part and to a varying extent, from one individual to another, by these circumstances. In view of how rarely men of wealth and high social standing turn out to be critics of the prevailing order, it seems a fair inference that their love of the way things are owes something to how well things are for them. Some men born to advantages, perhaps influenced by a great teacher, a book, a shattering experience, their own sensitivity, or by a combination of these and other factors, become critical of the very social order under which they have thrived because they are outraged by how many people, through no fault of their own, fare dismally under that order. The presidents were not such men.

A close reading of their biographies and their utterances leaves the impression that those who grew up amidst unusually favorable circumstances somehow learned to regard both their good fortune and the social arrangements responsible for it not only as the way things are but as the way things ought to be. And those who attained great success largely on their own were similarly disposed toward an order flexible enough to permit the virtuous and the talented to rise from obscurity to its most exalted ranks. The only division in their social thinking was not between conservatives and radicals, for they were all conservative, but between the great majority of them who appear to have been totally indifferent to inequities or the plight of have-nots and the few who were sensitive to the need for reform. Even in the absence of definitive proof, it does seem reasonable to conclude that their privileged social origins and backgrounds played a significant part in shaping the ideologically conservative social philosophies and political policies of the presidents.

That the major parties have sought presidential candidates of sound social mind rather than high promise of statesmanship says something disconcerting about American politics and the American political system. It indicates that for all the 4th of July oratory glorifying the great office and proclaiming its importance, the men who have run things politically do not think the presidency really matters very much. Otherwise, why would they so often have chosen candidates so obviously lacking in greatness?

Perhaps it is more accurate to suggest that our politicos do think that the office matters but they have been less than frank in explaining *how* they think it matters. For, while the public has been led to think that precisely because the office is so great and so crucial it must be filled by men of outstanding ability, party leaders—perhaps because they know how important the office might be as pulpit for and symbol of humanitarian reform and far-reaching social change—have sought to fill it with men unsympathetic to such change. Not accidentally, such men have been lesser men—at least when measured by standards of intellect, learning, statecraft, and wisdom, rather than by worldly success alone. That a Lincoln or an FDR, on reaching the White House, turned out to be wiser than anyone had the right to expect does not detract from the force of this general rule that the parties are cheerfully ready to forgo greatness for soundness.

The evidence suggests that the American political system is more ideological than the conventional scholarly wisdom likes to think it is. In avoiding extremists and men whose principles and ideals, no matter how morally admirable, are certain to evoke strong and even bitter controversy and opposition, our major parties, we are told, manifest their sensible practicality, their aversion to inflaming the emotions of the electorate. Seeking control, as they do, of the center that usually holds the balance of power in American politics, the great parties supposedly display their preference for pragmatism over ideological extremism. What this analysis overlooks is that the center is no less a position on the ideological spectrum than any other. Parties that were truly unideological would judge candidates by their ability, their promise, their integrity of character. It is because our parties are as strenuously ideological as they in fact are that they brush merit aside and focus rather on their candidates' ideological convictions. That our truly ideological parties are widely believed to be *un*ideological testifies both to the great success they have enjoyed in propagating yet another myth and to Americans' fumbling grasp of a concept—ideology—that we like to believe is nonexistent in our politics just as class is supposedly nonexistent in our society.

The social and economic atypicality of the presidents raises questions about the nature of democracy in the United States or, more particularly, about the extent to which we are a social democracy. For in the politics of a true social democracy, one would expect to find the highest office occupied by men and women who represent a cross section of the society, socially and occupationally. The intelligence and other qualities ideally required of a political leader would seem to be as available among skilled mechanics, farmers, teachers, and architects as among politicians and lawyers; no less common among men or women of modest income than among the unusually well-to-do. That we have actually selected our presidential candidates almost entirely from the upper levels of the social order leaves the disconcerting impression that our politics are concerned excessively with serving, not the general interests of the people as a whole, but the narrow interests of the small privileged and wealthy minority. However one explains it, the unrelenting nonrepresentation in the highest office of people of the incomes, wealth levels, and occupations that have predominated in our society throughout our history is not a statistical accident, devoid of significance. It signifies rather that the people who rule are not *the people.*

Perhaps the most disquieting implication of the evidence follows from the acute significance that attaches to the American presidency in the nuclear age. Without our willing it to be so, the American chief executive has come to have a life and death power over the future not of Americans alone but of all humanity. A decent respect to the opinion and needs of mankind requires that we seek in the future, as we have not sought in the past, to select candidates of commanding intelligence, learning, and above all patience, wisdom, and humanity—traits all that are not necessarily revealed by high social standing and the ideological preferences that typically accompany such standing.

Bibliographical Note

There is a vast literature on the presidents and the presidency. This note is confined to writings that I found particularly useful or appropriate to the themes of this book. And since I have compared the social standing of the presidents and their families with the standing of the American people, from George Washington's time to the present, I have thought it helpful to include writings on class and the American social or class structure.

Discussions and interpretations of the presidency that I have drawn on include Thomas A. Bailey, *Presidential Greatness: The Image and the Man from George Washington to the Present* (New York, 1966); James David Barber, *The Presidential Character: Predicting Performance in the White House,* 2nd ed. (Engelwood Cliffs, 1977); James Bryce, *The American Commonwealth,* 2 vols. (New York, 1888); Edward S. Corwin, *The Presidency, Office and Powers, 1787–1957,* 4th rev. ed. (New York, 1957); Edward S. Corwin, and Louis W. Koenig, *The Presidency Today* (New York, 1956); Marcus Cunliffe, *American Presidents and the Presidency* (London, 1969); Herman Finer, *The Presidency: Crisis and Regeneration, An Essay in Possibilities* (Chicago, 1960); Sidney Hyman, *The American President* (New York, 1954); Louis W. Koenig, *The Chief Executive* (New York, 1964); Harold J. Laski, *The American Presidency: An Interpretation* (New York, 1940); Stefan Lorant, *The Glorious Burden: The American Presidency* (New York, 1968); Richard E. Neustadt, *Presidential Power: The Politics of Leadership* (New York, 1960); George E. Reedy, *The Twilight of the*

Presidency (New York, 1970); and Clinton Rossiter, *The American Presidency,* rev. ed. (New York, 1960).

Valuable biographies, autobiographies, and private writings of the presidents (in chronological order, beginning with Washington) include James Thomas Flexner, *George Washington: The Forge of Experience* (Boston, 1965); Douglas S. Freeman, *George Washington, A Biography,* 7 vols. (New York, 1948–57); L. H. Butterfield, ed., *The Adams Papers: Diary and Autobiography of John Adams,* 4 vols. (Cambridge, Mass., 1962); Page Smith, *John Adams,* 2 vols. (Garden City, N.Y., 1962); Dumas Malone, *Jefferson and His Time,* 5 vols. (Boston, 1948–74); Irving Brant, *James Madison,* 6 vols. (Indianapolis, 1941–61); Harry Ammon, *James Monroe: The Quest for National Identity* (New York, 1971); William P. Cresson, *James Monroe* (Chapel Hill, 1946); Samuel Flagg Bemis, *John Quincy Adams and The Foundations of American Foreign Policy* (New York, 1965); Marie B. Hecht, *John Quincy Adams: A Personal History of an Independent Man* (New York, 1972); Allan Nevins, ed., *The Diary of John Quincy Adams, 1794–1845* (New York, 1951); John Spencer Bassett, *The Life of Andrew Jackson,* 2 vols. (New York, 1931); John Spencer Bassett, ed., *Correspondence of Andrew Jackson,* 7 vols. (Washington, 1926–35); Marquis James, *The Life of Andrew Jackson,* 2 vols. (Indianapolis, 1933, 1938); James Parton, *Life of Andrew Jackson* (New York, 1860); Robert V. Remini, *Andrew Jackson and the Course of American Empire* and *Andrew Jackson and the Course of American Freedom* (New York, 1977, 1981); Donald B. Cole, *The Little Magician* [Van Buren] (Princeton, forthcoming); Denis Tilden Lynch, *An Epoch and a Man: Martin Van Buren and His Times* (New York, 1929); John Niven, *Martin Van Buren and the Romantic Age of American Politics* (Oxford, forthcoming); Edward M. Shepard, *Martin Van Buren* (Boston, 1890); Martin Van Buren, *The Autobiography of Martin Van Buren* (Washington, 1918); Freeman Cleaves, *Old Tippecanoe: William Henry Harrison and His Time* (New York, 1939); Dorothy Burne Goebel, *William Henry Harrison: A Political Biography* (Philadelphia, 1974); Oliver Perry Chitwood, *John Tyler, Champion of the Old South* (New York, 1939); Robert Seager II, *And Tyler Too: A Biography of John and Julia Gardiner Tyler* (New York, 1963); Eugene I. McCormick, *James K. Polk: A Political Biography* (New York, 1965); Allan Nevins, ed., *The Diary of a President, 1845–1849* (London, 1929); Charles Sellers, *James K. Polk: Jacksonian, 1795–1843* and *James K. Polk: Continentalist, 1843–1846* (Princeton, 1957, 1966); Holman Hamilton, *Zachary Taylor; Soldier of the Republic* and *Zachary Taylor: Soldier in the White House* (Hamden, Conn., 1966); Millard Fillmore, "The Early History of Hon. Millard

Fillmore (Written by Himself)," *Publication of the Buffalo Historical Society,* II (Buffalo, 1880); Robert J. Rayback, *Millard Fillmore: Biography of a President* (Buffalo, 1959); Nathaniel Hawthorne, *Life of Franklin Pierce* (Boston, 1852); Roy Franklin Nichols, *Franklin Pierce: Young Hickory of the Granite Hills* (Philadelphia, 1931); George Ticknor Curtis, *Life of James Buchanan,* 2 vols. (New York, 1883); Philip Shriver Klein, *President James Buchanan: A Biography* (University Park, Pa., 1962); Stephen B. Oates, *With Malice toward None: The Life of Abraham Lincoln* (New York, 1977); Carl Sandburg, *Abraham Lincoln: The Prairie Years,* and *Abraham Lincoln: The War Years* (New York, 1926, 1939); Benjamin P. Thomas, *Abraham Lincoln, A Biography* (New York, 1962); Lloyd P. Stryker, *Andrew Johnson: A Study in Courage* (New York, 1929); Lately Thomas, *The First President Johnson: The Three Lives of the Seventeenth President of the United States* (New York, 1968); Robert W. Winton, *Andrew Johnson, Plebeian and Patriot* (New York, 1928); William B. Hesseltine, *Ulysses S. Grant, Politician* (New York, 1935); Lloyd Lewis, *Captain Sam Grant* (Boston, 1950); William S. McFeely, *Grant: A Biography* (New York, 1981); W. E. Woodward, *Meet General Grant* (New York, 1928); Harry Barnard, *Rutherford B. Hayes and His America* (Indianapolis, 1954); H. J. Eckenrode, *Rutherford B. Hayes: Statesman of Reunion* (New York, 1930); Robert Granville Caldwell, *James A. Garfield: Party Chieftain* (New York, 1931); Allan Peskin, *Garfield* (Kent, Ohio, 1978); John Clark Ridpath, *The Life and Work of James A. Garfield* (New York, 1882); Theodore Clarke Smith, *The Life and Letters of James A. Garfield,* 2 vols. (New Haven, 1925); George Frederick Howe, *Chester A. Arthur, A Quarter-Century of Machine Politics* (New York, 1935); Thomas C. Reeves, *Gentleman Boss: The Life of Chester Alan Arthur* (New York, 1975); Allan Nevins, *Grover Cleveland, A Study in Courage* (New York, 1932); Harry Sievers, *Benjamin Harrison,* 3 vols. (Indianapolis, 1952–68); Margaret Leech, *In the Days of McKinley* (New York, 1959); Charles S. Olcott, *The Life of William McKinley,* 2 vols. (Boston, 1916); William Henry Harbaugh, *Power and Responsibility: The Life and Time of Theodore Roosevelt* (New York, 1961); David McCullough, *Mornings on Horseback* (New York, 1981); Edmund Morris, *The Rise of Theodore Roosevelt* (New York, 1979); Henry F. Pringle, *Theodore Roosevelt: A Biography* (New York, 1931); Herbert S. Duffy, *William Howard Taft* (New York, 1930); Henry F. Pringle, *The Life and Times of William Howard Taft, A Biography,* 2 vols. (New York, 1939); Ray Stannard Baker, *Woodrow Wilson: Life and Letters,* 5 vols. (Garden City, 1927); Arthur Link, *Wilson,* 5 vols. (Princeton, 1947–65); Eleanor Wilson McAdoo, *The Woodrow Wilsons* (New York, 1937);

Gene Smith, *When the Cheering Stopped: The Last Years of Woodrow Wilson* (New York, 1964); Samuel Hopkins Adams, *Incredible Era: The Life and Times of Warren Gamaliel Harding* (Boston, 1939); Randolph C. Downes, *The Rise of Warren Gamaliel Harding, 1865–1920* (Columbus, 1970); Francis Russell, *The Shadow of Blooming Grove: Warren G. Harding and His Times* (New York, 1968); Andrew Sinclair, *The Available Man: The Life Behind the Masks of Warren Gamaliel Harding* (New York, 1965); Calvin Coolidge, *The Autobiography of Calvin Coolidge* (New York, 1929); Donald R. McCoy, *Calvin Coolidge, The Quiet President* (New York, 1967); William Allen White, *Calvin Coolidge, The Man Who Is President* (New York, 1925); William Allen White, *A Puritan in Babylon: The Story of Calvin Coolidge* (New York, 1938); David Burner, *Herbert Hoover, A Public Life* (New York, 1979); Herbert Clark Hoover, *Memoirs*, 3 vols. (New York, 1951–52); Eugene Lyons, *Herbert Hoover, A Biography* (Garden City, 1964); Joan Hoff Wilson, *Herbert Hoover, Forgotten Progressive* (Boston, 1975); Frank B. Freidel, *Franklin D. Roosevelt*, 3 vols. (Boston, 1952–56); Arthur M. Schlesinger, Jr., *The Age of Roosevelt*, 2 vols. (Boston, 1957–59); Bert Cochran, *Harry Truman and the Crisis Presidency* (New York, 1973); Jonathan Daniels, *The Man of Independence* (Philadelphia, 1950); Alfred Steinberg, *The Man from Missouri: The Life and Times of Harry S. Truman* (New York, 1962); Harry S. Truman, *Memoirs* (Garden City, 1955); Margaret Truman, *Harry S. Truman* (New York, 1973); Kenneth S. Davis, *Soldier of Democracy, A Biography of Dwight Eisenhower* (Garden City, 1945); Peter Lyon, *Eisenhower: Portrait of the Hero* (Boston, 1974); Herbert S. Parmet, *Eisenhower and the American Crusades* (New York, 1972); James McGregor Burns, *John Kennedy: A Political Portrait* (New York, 1959); William R. Manchester, *Portrait of a President: John F. Kennedy in Profile* (Boston, 1962); Herbert S. Parmet, *Jack: The Struggles of John F. Kennedy* (New York, 1980); Arthur M. Schlesinger, Jr., *A Thousand Days: John F. Kennedy in the White House* (Boston, 1965); Hugh Sidey, *John F. Kennedy, President* (New York, 1963); Theodore C. Sorenson, *Kennedy* (New York, 1965); Richard J. Whalen, *The Founding Father: The Story of Joseph P. Kennedy* (New York, 1964); Robert A. Caro, *The Years of Lyndon Johnson* (New York, 1982); Ronnie Dugger, *The Politician: The Life and Times of Lyndon—The Drive for Power, From the Frontier to Master of the Senate* (New York, 1982); Doris Kearns, *Lyndon Johnson and the American Dream* (New York, 1976); David Abrahamsen, *Nixon vs. Nixon: An Emotional Tragedy* (New York, 1976); Leonard Lurie, *The Running of Richard Nixon* (New York, 1972); Earl Mazo, *Richard Nixon: A Political and Personal Portrait* (New York, 1959); Ralph W. Toledano, *One Man Alone: Richard Nixon*

(New York, 1969); Clark R. Mollenhoff, *The Man Who Pardoned Nixon* (New York, 1976); Jerald F. terHorst, *Gerald Ford and the Future of the Presidency* (New York, 1974); Jimmy Carter, *Why Not the Best?* (Nashville, 1975); Tom Collins, *The Search for Jimmy Carter* (Waco, 1976); David Kucharsky, *The Man from Plains: The Mind and Spirit of Jimmy Carter* (New York, 1976); Leslie Wheeler, *Jimmy Who? An Examination of the Presidential Candidate Jimmy Carter: The Man, His Career, His Stand on the Issues* (Woodbury, N.Y., 1976); Bill Boyarsky, *The Rise of Ronald Reagan* (New York, 1968); Edmund G. (Pat) Brown and Bill Brown, *Reagan the Political Chameleon* (New York, 1976); Laurence Leamer, *Make-Believe: The Story of Nancy and Ronald Reagan* (New York, 1983); Joseph Lewis, *What Makes Reagan Run? A Political Profile* (New York, 1968); and Ronald Reagan (with Richard G. Hubler), *Where's the Rest of Me?* (New York, 1965).

I have gathered diverse facts about the presidency and the men occupying the office from Dorothy Burne Goebel and Julius Goebel, Jr., *Generals in the White House* (New York, 1945); Joseph Nathan Kane, *Facts about the Presidents; A Compilation of Biographical and Historical Data* (New York, 1968); National Survey of Historic Sites and Buildings, *The Presidents: From the Inauguration of George Washington to the Inauguration of Jimmy Carter (Historic Places Commemorating the Chief Executives of the United States*, rev. ed. (Washington, 1977); Henry L. Stoddard, *It Costs To Be President* (New York, 1938); Tim Taylor, *The Book of Presidents* (New York, 1972); and David C. Whitney, *The Presidents: Biographies of the Chief Executives from Washington through Reagan* (Garden City, 1982).

Miscellaneous evidence on presidential attributes and characteristics can be found in Maxim E. Armbruster, *The Presidents of the United States: A New Appraisal, From Washington to Kennedy*, rev. ed. (New York, 1963); Robert J. Evans, "The Educational Backgrounds of the Presidents of the United States," *Dauphin County Historical Review* 9 (December 1961): 13–19; John Frost, *The Presidents of the United States from Washington to Cleveland, Comprising Their Personal and Political History* (Boston, 1899); Reginald Buchanan Henry, *Genealogies of the Families of the Presidents* (Rutland, Vt., 1935); Cranston Jones, *Homes of the American Presidents* (New York, 1962); Herman H. Kohlsaat, *From McKinley to Harding: Personal Recollections of Our Presidents* (New York, 1928); A. K. McClure, *Our Presidents and How We Make Them* (New York, 1900); Bessie White Smith, *The Boyhoods of the Presidents* (Boston, 1929) and *The Romances of the Presidents* (Boston, 1932); Gilson Willets, *Inside History of the White House: The Complete History of the Domestic and Official Life in Washington of the*

Nation's Presidents and Their Families (New York, 1908); James Grant Wilson, ed., *The Presidents of the United States, 1789–1894* (New York, 1894); John Sergeant Wise, *Recollections of Thirteen Presidents* (1906; reprint, Freeport, N.Y., 1968); and Simon Wolf, *The Presidents I Have Known from 1860–1918* (Washington, 1918).

For the public addresses of most of the presidents see James D. Richardson, ed., *A Compilation of the Messages and Papers of the Presidents, 1789–1902,* 11 vols. (Washington, 1896–1902). For the religion of the presidents see Edmund Fuller and David E. Green, *God in the White House: The Faiths of American Presidents* (New York, 1968); and Bliss Isely, *The Presidents: Men of Faith* (Boston, 1953).

For evidence on the wives and mothers of the presidents I have read Doris Faber, *The Mothers of American Presidents* (New York, 1968); William Judson Hampton, *Our Presidents and Their Mothers* (Boston, 1922); Laura C. Holloway, *The Ladies of the White House, or, In the Homes of the Presidents* (Philadelphia, 1882); Joseph P. Lash, *Eleanor and Franklin* (New York, 1971); Jane and Burt McConnell, *First Ladies from Martha Washington to Mamie Eisenhower* (New York, 1953); Marianne Means, *The Woman in the White House: The Lives, Times, and Influence of Twelve Notable First Ladies* (New York, 1963); Ishbel Ross, *Grace Coolidge and Her Era: The Story of a President's Wife* (New York, 1962); and Harriet Upton, *Our Early Presidents, Their Wives and Children* (Boston, 1890).

A clearer perspective on the presidency is afforded by discussions of political elites in general. I have profited from Charles A. Beard, *The Economic Basis of Politics* (New York, 1957); T. B. Bottomore, *Elites and Society* (Middlesex, Eng., 1964); Philip H. Burch, Jr., *Elites in American History,* 3 vols. (New York, 1980); G. William Domhoff, *Who Rules America?* (Engelwood Cliffs, 1967) and *Who Really Rules? New Haven and Community Power Reexamined* (Santa Monica, 1978); Thomas R. Dye, *Who's Running America? Institutional Leadership in the United States* (Engelwood Cliffs, 1976); Heinz Eulau, *Class and Party in the Eisenhower Years: Class Roles and Perspectives in the 1952 and 1956 Elections* (Glencoe, Ill., 1962); Richard F. Hamilton, *Class and Politics in the United States* (New York, 1972); Hugh Heclo, "Presidential and Prime Ministerial Selection," in Donald R. Matthews, ed., *Perspectives on Presidential Selection* (Washington, 1973), pp. 19–48; Suzanne Keller, *Beyond the Ruling Class: Strategic Elites in Modern Society* (New York, 1963); Harold Lasswell and Abraham Kaplan, *Power and Society: A Framework for Political Inquiry* (New Haven, 1950); Dwayne Marvick, ed., *Political Decision-Makers* (Glencoe, Ill., 1961); Donald R. Matthews, *The Social Backgrounds of Political Deci-*

sion-Makers (New York, 1954); Robert Michels, *Political Parties: A Sociological Study of the Oligarchical Tendencies of Modern Democracy* (Glencoe, Ill., 1949); and Kenneth Prewitt and Alan Stone, *The Ruling Elites: Elite Theory, Power, and American Democracy* (New York, 1973). Also bearing on the theme is Edward Pessen, "Social Structure and Politics in American History," *American Historical Review* 87 (December 1982): 1290–1325.

Useful theoretical discussion and evidence on the American social or class structure are included in Jerold S. Auerbach, *Unequal Justice: Lawyers and Social Change in Modern America* (New York, 1976); E. Digby Baltzell, *The Protestant Establishment: Aristocracy and Caste in America* (London, 1965) and *Puritan Boston and Quaker Philadelphia: Two Protestant Ethics and the Spirit of Class Authority and Leadership* (New York, 1979); Bernard Barber, *Social Stratification: A Comparative Analysis of Structure and Process* (New York, 1957); Daniel Bell, *The Coming of Post-Industrial Society: A Venture in Social Forecasting* (New York, 1976); Reinhard Bendix and Seymour Martin Lipset, eds., *Class, Status, and Power: Social Stratification in Comparative Perspective* (New York, 1966); Peter M. Blau, ed., *Approaches to the Study of Social Structure* (New York, 1975); Ralf Dahrendorf, *Class and Class Conflict in Industrial Society* (Stanford, 1959); David L. Featherman and Robert M. Hauser, "Changes in the Socioeconomic Stratification of the Races, 1962–73," *American Journal of Sociology* 82 (November 1976): 621–51; Anthony Giddens, *The Class Structure of the Advanced Societies* (New York, 1973); David Gottlieb and Jay Campbell, Jr., "Winners and Losers in the Race for the Good Life: A Comparison of Blacks and Whites," *Social Science Quarterly* 49 (December 1968): 593–602; Harold Hodges, *Social Stratification: Class in America* (Cambridge, Mass., 1969); Joseph A. Kahl, *The American Class Structure* (New York, 1957); Gerhard E. Lenski, *Power and Privilege: A Theory of Social Stratification* (New York, 1966); Robert S. Lynd and Helen Merrill Lynd, *Middletown: A Study in Contemporary American Culture* (New York, 1929); Jackson T. Main, *The Social Structure of Revolutionary America* (Princeton, 1965); Robert K. Merton, *Social Theory and Social Structure,* rev. ed. (Glencoe, Ill., 1957); Herman P. Miller, *Rich Man, Poor Man* (New York, 1964); William C. Miller, ed., *Men in Business: Essays in the Historical Role of the Entrepreneur* (New York, 1962); Office of Federal Statistical Policy and Standards of the Department of Commerce, *Social Indicators, 1976* (Washington, 1977); Richard Parker, *The Myth of the Middle Class: Notes on Affluence and Equality* (New York, 1972); Edward Pessen, *Riches, Class, and Power Before the Civil War* (Lexington,

Mass., 1973); Edward Pessen, ed., *Three Centuries of Social Mobility in America* (Lexington, Mass., 1974); Richard Polenberg, *One Nation Divisible: Class, Race, and Ethnicity in the United States Since 1938* (New York, 1980); Leonard Riessman, *Class in American Society* (New York, 1959); Jonathan H. Turner and Charles E. Starnes, *Inequality, Privilege, and Poverty in America* (Pacific Palisades, Cal., 1976); United States Bureau of the Census, *Historical Statistics of the United States*, 2 vols. (Washington, 1975); W. Lloyd Warner and Paul S. Lunt, *The Social Life of a Modern Community* (New Haven, 1941); and Maurice Zeitlin, ed., *Classes, Class Conflict, and the State: Empirical Studies in Class Analysis* (Cambridge, Mass., 1980).

Index